estherpress

Books for Courageous Women

ESTHER PRESS VISION

Publishing diverse voices that encourage and equip women to walk courageously in the light of God's truth for such a time as this.

BIBLICAL STATEMENT OF PURPOSE

"For if you keep silent at this time, relief and deliverance will rise for the Jews from another place, but you and your father's house will perish. And who knows whether you have not come to the kingdom for such a time as this?"

Esther 4:14 (ESV)

What people are saying about ...

GOD'S GOT YOU

"The title alone grabbed my attention. *God's Got You*? Yes, please! What I found inside was page after page of encouragement, understanding, and spiritual direction—what we all need when it's time to begin anew. Tracie writes from a place of empathy and experience, carefully crafting her words to speak directly to our hearts. Her advice is both practical and sound, as she urges us to 'dream big, start small.' So wise. If it's courage you need, beloved, you've found the perfect resource."

Liz Curtis Higgs, bestselling author
of *Bad Girls of the Bible*

"In *God's Got You*, Tracie helps you navigate the bumpy roads of change— wiping the fog of fear from your eyes, calming the emotional chaos of uncertainty, and steering you down the path of new beginnings. You'll discover a courage and confidence you never thought you'd have again."

Sharon Jaynes, bestselling author of 26 books
including *Praying for Your Child from Head to Toe* and
Enough: Silencing the Lies That Steal Your Confidence

"If you are feeling disillusioned and defeated because life has thrown you for a loop, or if you're feeling stuck, longing to move in a new direction but clueless as to how to start, *God's Got You* is the guidebook you need. Tracie Miles has crafted a practical and biblical resource that will enable you to stop feeling fearful and frustrated and become a woman who is courageously secure. Armed with a new perspective—and strengthened with timeless truths from Scripture—you will go forth in spiritual confidence and find your life renewed."

Karen Ehman, *New York Times*–bestselling
author of 21 books including *When Making Others Happy Is Making You Miserable* and *Keep It Shut*

"In *God's Got You*, author Tracie Miles lays out the roadmap we need to push through the fog and walk into the future with a new perspective and a clear mind. Tracie's hard-earned wisdom will meet you where you are and provide the momentum you need to keep going—one practical, life-giving step at a time. With refreshing transparency and the grace we need when embracing new beginnings, Tracie comes alongside us as an empathic friend who understands what it's like to be stuck and what it takes to move forward into abundance. So if you're ready to kick fear to the curb and let God take your life to the next level, then it's *time* to grab this book and start the journey!"

Meredith Houston Carr, JD, speaker,
writer for Proverbs 31 Ministries
Encouragement for Today devotions

"If you are facing a new beginning, then this book is for you! In *God's Got You*, Tracie writes from a place of wisdom and experience as she provides practical steps to help you regain your confidence and courage. This book is a perfect guide and source of encouragement filled with biblical insight and comfort for anyone facing unwanted or unexpected change. You can be assured: God's got you!"

Courtney Joseph Fallick, writer at WomenLivingWell.org (Good Morning Girls), author of *Still Standing*

"Tracie is the cherished friend coming alongside to pick us up and begin again when life simply hurts. She instills the courage to believe that just because we don't like where we are does not mean it is not the best place to begin again; with the foundation already laid, it is not a waste. It isn't new surroundings that will change us when unanticipated lifequakes happen ... but a new mindset. Tracie beautifully infuses Scriptures into every principle she shares as she leads us to let go of what we *knew* to embrace the *new*. Seeing the bigger picture helps us begin with the end in mind: God does not leave us in a holding pattern, and He makes all things new."

Denise Pass, PhD in Biblical Exposition at Liberty University, author of *Make Up Your Mind*

Other Books by Tracie Miles

Tracie Miles

GOD'S

Embracing New Beginnings

GOT

with Courage and Confidence

YOU

estherpress

Books for Courageous Women
from David C Cook

GOD'S GOT YOU
Published by Esther Press,
an imprint of David C Cook
4050 Lee Vance Drive
Colorado Springs, CO 80918 U.S.A.

Integrity Music Limited, a Division of David C Cook
Brighton, East Sussex BN1 2RE, England

Library of Congress Control Number 2023948796
ISBN 978-0-8307-8098-3
eISBN 978-0-8307-8114-0

The Team: Susan McPherson, Alice Crider, Stephanie Bennett, Judy Gillispie,
Kayla Fenstermaker, James Hershberger, Susan Murdock
Cover Design: Brian Mellema

Printed in the United States of America
First Edition 2024

1 2 3 4 5 6 7 8 9 10

040524

Contents

A Note from Tracie

When we go through any major life transition, our hearts can become unsettled and our minds may grapple for answers. We long to be successful and have courage and faith to persevere, but we often secretly wonder if we have what it takes to push forward into new and uncertain territory.

Possibly you're facing a new season of life because of circumstances beyond your control—an empty nest, a divorce, the death of your spouse, going back to work after years of staying home raising children, midlife, a new job, a relocation, or a new home.

Maybe you've put so much emotional investment, effort, or time into where you are now that you wonder if it's even worth it to try to begin again. To reinvent yourself. To reshape your life. To start fresh when it seems so much of life has already passed. You might be doubting if true growth and unlimited possibilities can be part of your story at this stage of life.

Maybe you have a dream sprouting in your heart but you're afraid to take a risk, lacking the self-confidence to pursue it while feeling incapable and unworthy. Maybe you feel consumed with a paralyzing fear of taking chances and failing. It may be that the COVID pandemic a few years ago turned your life upside down, leaving you still scrambling to fix the mess it left behind—financial ruin, job displacement, lost loved ones, medical problems, substance abuse issues, or weight gain.

You long to invent the new you, or reinvent yourself altogether, but fear and a lack of self-confidence are like anchors tied to your feet, keeping you from making progress. All the what-ifs are haunting your heart like nobody's business.

No matter what circumstances have led you to this crossroads, you may find yourself lying awake at night with worrisome thoughts running rampant. *How did I end up here? Why do I feel like I'm back at square one? How am I supposed to start over? Can I actually launch something fresh or go in a brand-new direction? Should I even try to begin again?*

Unfortunately, these questions and big decisions can feel like black clouds hanging over our heads, preventing us from seeing all the possibilities life holds and keeping us stuck where we are.

The truth is, if God has planted a seed in our hearts—a longing to do something new, big, adventurous, risky, or just out of the norm—then He has equipped us to do exactly that. If He has allowed a situation or season to come into our lives, then He has qualified us to handle it in His strength and given us all we need.

But how do we know how and when to move forward, and how can we trust that this *new* we're longing for will work out?

The solution to finding the courage and desire to take that leap of faith to reinvent ourselves and our lives is to recognize there is a huge difference between starting over and beginning again.

Beginning again doesn't mean starting over from scratch with no foundation, knowledge, or resources. We all possess memories and experiences to lean on. We have gained wisdom and learned lessons, which have brought us to where we are today. We have developed skills and relationships, endured failures and disappointments, and enjoyed triumphs and successes. We have a story and have lived many chapters of life. We all have a past, yet we aren't the same people we were in the past, so we aren't starting in the same place we've ever started before.

In fact, we aren't actually *starting over*; we're simply beginning again in a new place in life. We're beginning anew in the place God has us right now. A place He has held our hand and walked us to, a place He has prepared for us and prepared us for long ago, and a place in which He has already equipped us to rise up, conquer, and succeed.

We're going to explore so many things together in this book, and I can only wish I could hear your enthusiasm about all the possibilities for your life when you finish here. We're going to talk about getting through the hardest of seasons, overcoming stumbling blocks, defining specific goals for your personal journey, making a life plan that works, embracing change, and finding the courage and confidence to take chances.

I want to help you find your people—the ones who can't wait to cheer you on—along with the faith to keep going when you feel like you're failing. I want to instill in you the perseverance and persistence you need to never give up so that you can start making things happen once and for all—for you.

Before you read any farther, friend, I need you to know one very important thing. I'm not writing this book from the standpoint of "I came and I conquered! Hooray for me!" No. Rather, I'm writing from a place of struggle. Currently hunkered down in the bunker of a major transitional period in my own life, in more ways than one. As I get a little more personal with you in the next few chapters, you'll understand, and we're going to be buds.

Regardless of why you may be struggling, we're in this together now, and you and I can and will come out on top if we believe in ourselves and our God, who is our ever-present help.

I know believing in ourselves—and the *new* that God has for us— doesn't always come naturally. I also know sometimes the road ahead looks so foggy, scary, and treacherous that we can't find the determination to drive through it with peace and unwavering faith.

Yet that is what must be done. When we're willing and eager to change our situation or, at a minimum, our perspective and move forward in faith, the changes we desire can and will occur.

God has already given us the ability to carry out even our biggest dreams and make it through hard transitions. We simply must be willing to trust Him, muster up our courage, push past doubts, find the courage to take that chance, and expect nothing but the best.

When we accept we're in a stage of life in which profound growth and change have happened and intentionally cling to the belief that we can do whatever we feel called to do through the power of Christ, we can become willing and even excited to start the true adventure of beginning again.

You've got this because God's got you. Now let's get moving.

Tracie

Chapter 1

When You Can't See through the Fog

If you want a new beginning, you just have to begin.

One day years ago, I was full of emotions as I drove to pick up my dad for a major surgery that he was scheduled for later that morning. The closer I got to his house, the tighter the knot forming in the pit of my stomach became. I was filled with anxiety, knowing we could receive very bad news from the surgeon. Hot tears began stinging my eyes.

Then suddenly, through those tears, I saw a man in the fog.

Due to the limited visibility, I was driving unusually slowly down my dad's street when I noticed the figure in the distance walking straight toward me. I thought it was quite peculiar for anyone to be walking outside so early, but as I got closer, my eyes widened and my heart began to pound.

The figure began to resemble a silhouette of someone I immediately recognized—someone who shouldn't be standing in the middle of the road on a foggy morning. As I approached him, I could see he had on a soft white shirt and baggy tan pants, his bare feet sticking out from the bottom as he carried his brown sandals in his hand. He appeared to be in his midthirties, with wavy brown hair and a full beard, although he had a neatly kept appearance.

He looked exactly like Jesus—like all those drawings in children's Bible storybooks. And he was now oddly standing right in front of my dad's house.

My heart skipped a beat. My thoughts raced. My mind knew Jesus Christ wouldn't be standing in front of a house in a small beach town in North Carolina, but my heart told me He was indeed there.

I could not take my eyes off him. Chill bumps covered my body from head to toe. As I crept past him and pulled into the driveway, his eyes met mine for a split second and a sweet, gentle smile washed over his face. Then he nodded and disappeared into the fog.

I sat in my car somewhat stunned. For one moment, it had felt as if I were looking into the eyes of Jesus. A sense of peace flooded my spirit. It was as if God's quiet whisper penetrated my heart, assuring me that, regardless of the outcome, everything would be okay even though the healing journey for my dad would be long. Throughout that day at the hospital, I couldn't get the man in the fog out of my head. I truly felt as if I had experienced a Jesus encounter, and He was right by my side all day long.

Now I'm not saying I actually saw Jesus, of course, but I do believe He divinely designed that meeting in the road and orchestrated it as a sign that I would recognize. I think He intended to saturate my heart with the reminder that He really does walk among us and He is always with us in every situation, especially those in which our hearts are heavy and burdened with unknowns. In a very tangible way, Jesus showed me He understands my fears and He cares. I think He also knew I really needed to "see" Him that day.

Jesus Cares about You Too

Jesus also cares about you today. Standing there in a stare-down with the unknowns of your future, lost in the fog of a life that used to feel so clear.

Maybe you're wrestling with swirling thoughts like these:

I feel stuck where I am, and I want to start something new. I have big dreams and ideas, and I want to turn my visions into reality. But can I? Do I have what it takes? And where would I even begin?

I'm not where I thought I would be at this age. All my friends are married or having babies, and I'm still stuck and disappointed in myself and my circumstances.

I'm turning fifty? My life is nothing like I thought it would look, but is it too late to start anew?

I never wanted to get divorced, but now I'm alone, afraid, and forced to start over, yet I have no idea how to move forward. Or if I even can.

All my children have now moved out, are married, and have lives of their own. What am I supposed to do with myself?

Why did God allow this transition in my life? I'm kind of mad at Him and doubting His goodness, but I'm afraid to let anyone know how I really feel.

If any of those thoughts sound familiar to you or if a unique opportunity or struggle relevant to you just popped into your mind after reading these, I can only assume that, for some reason, you're in uncharted territory in the landscape of your life.

You're in a phase of transition, wondering how to manage your emotions or control your negative thoughts about this unfamiliar and uncomfortable place you've found yourself in. Not knowing whether to turn left or right—or how to turn in any direction for that matter. Uncertain about where to find solutions or how to bring about change. Please know you are not alone.

From time to time, we all come up against fears of the unknown, transitional seasons of life, and personal problems that seem hopeless or scary. We all face seasons of new beginnings and unfamiliar shifts in our lives that can feel beyond our ability to handle, no matter how big or small they may be.

During these journeys into our new seasons, it's easy to get caught up in our emotions and worries, let our fears get the better of us, and forget to look for Jesus amid the gloom. In some situations, we may even find ourselves wondering if He is even aware of our problems, if He sees the fog we're pushing through, and if He really cares about what we're enduring. But we never have to live afraid and alone.

Joshua 1:9 serves as a sweet reminder that Jesus is aware of what we're facing, He does care about what we're going through, and He is with us all the time: "This is my command—be strong and courageous! Do not be afraid or discouraged. For the LORD your God is with you wherever you go." Believing this promise will give you peace for the journey and is a great verse to tuck into your heart as you begin marching toward the new you.

Also keep in mind Proverbs 16:1: "The plans of the heart belong to man, but the answer of the tongue is from the LORD" (ESV). And Proverbs 16:9: "We can make our plans, but the LORD determines our steps." You see, the Lord gave us ears to hear Him, eyes to see Him, and a mind to plan out our lives, and He wants us to use them and be courageous while doing it, knowing He has our best interests in mind.

We're in This Together

As you walk through the rest of this book with me, I'm going to help you get through this season of new beginnings. No matter your current situation, the common denominator is the felt need we all share—the desire to be whole, secure, and happy in whatever phase of life we find ourselves in.

Regardless of our age or situation, if a lifequake of sorts happens—where everything seems shaken up, our circumstances drastically change, or seasons shift—it's normal to feel out of sorts as well. We feel directionless and confused, stuck in a place in a life we don't recognize and are unsure how to navigate. Fears and other emotions appear to be controlling our every waking moment, and as much as we want to feel and think differently, we simply don't know how.

We long to be successful and have the courage and faith to push through the forest of doubts in our minds and see even the smallest ray of hope shining through the trees, but we often feel lost, misplaced, and directionless. All of which causes us to secretly wonder if we even have what it takes to not only get through our unfamiliar, uncomfortable season but also come out on the other side feeling even better and happier than we did before.

Not only do we not feel like ourselves, but we don't even know who this "new me" is supposed to be now, much less how to survive and believe the future can be bright.

Even if you've been through no actual lifequake event, I bet you can still relate to these unspoken thoughts and feelings. You may question if the changes you're dreaming about and the visions of how you want your life to be are even possible. You may doubt if you even can begin again. Go for that scary yet exciting career move you've been dreaming about. Start that new business. Kick off a ministry idea God has been pricking your spirit about. Or write that book to share your story or start a blog or a podcast to encourage others.

Regardless of the circumstances that have led you to this crossroads, I imagine you don't want to be in such an uncertain position. You might feel angry about your situation—angry at God and even angry at yourself for being in this spot. If not angry, you might be frustrated at your own unwillingness to take a chance on yourself. Or maybe you're just plain ol' tired of feeling stuck and discontent, and you're ready for some adventure and excitement!

In any case, all these questions, thoughts, and feelings hold great power over our lives, our happiness, and our future, especially when we let them control us and dictate how we live out each day. They can be like a dense fog blurring our vision, preventing us from seeing all the possibilities and keeping us trapped where we are. All those exciting things we long for seem out of reach, and the courage to pursue them wanes when we get bogged down by the burdens of our transitions.

Yet you might agree that, despite your fear of beginning again, deep down *you still want to.*

Who wouldn't want a fresh start and new hope?

Perhaps you have a vision for what you want life to look like, who and how you want to be, but it seems like an out-of-reach fantasy. How can you know how and when to forge ahead? How can you trust that this *new* you're longing for or this *new* you were thrust into will actually work out in the long run? How can you overcome the obstacles keeping you from happiness? How can you start turning that fantasy of a better life into a reality?

How do you begin again?

It's Never Too Late

The truth is, if God has planted a seed in your heart—a desire to get through a change in your life with joy, a dream or vision, a longing to do something new, big, adventurous, risky, or just out of the norm—He is with you. If you're yearning to adopt a new outlook, tackle problems with courage and faith, or learn to acquire happiness right where you are, He has qualified you to do exactly that.

My friend, as I stated previously, God has already given you what you need. The qualifying and the equipping. And it's never too late to embrace a new beginning.

It's up to us to work on our confidence and courage (more on that coming up), remember our motivation and where we want to be, and then commit to persevere and succeed, while expecting nothing but God's best for us. We must stop worrying about what could go wrong and instead get excited about all that can go right!

It's never too late to embrace

a new beginning.

God-instilled power, confidence, and courage are inside you. You may just have to do the hard work to unearth them again! I promise you, if you do the work, God will bless the work, and you will be blessed. And eventually you're going to feel so proud of how far you've come!

These are all truths I remind myself of every day, especially when I'm feeling discouraged, afraid, or hopeless. I pray you will remember them too. It's not always easy and may at times feel impossible in the face of adversity, but take heart because, as Jesus promises us, "Humanly speaking, it is impossible. But with God everything is possible" (Matt. 19:26). For me and for you.

I came across a cute meme the other day that further supports this point: "It's impossible," said pride. "It's risky," said experience. "It's pointless," said reason. "Give it a try," whispered the heart. *Impossible, risky,* and *pointless* are all lies from the Enemy which can render us immobile and keep us from our new beginnings. They are not truths from God's Word, so let's not allow those thoughts to trip us up.

When we accept we're in a new stage of life—knowing profound growth and change have already happened, believing deeply in ourselves and our capabilities, and clinging to the truth that nothing is impossible with God—only then have we taken that first step toward the person we want to become or toward that place in life we know we want to land one day.

The new beginning you're heading toward may seem blurry right now. But transitioning well is simply the process of adapting to changes in life, whatever they may bring, and making the best of them.

You *can* reinvent yourself. You *can* reshape your life and your future. You *can* achieve the desires of your heart. And you *can* begin again. I'm learning to let the space between where I am and where I want to be inspire me and not terrify me. And I want to encourage you today to start doing the same.

Miracles will happen when we give as much energy to our dreams as we do our fears and inhibitions. Channel your energy into positive spaces, and I promise you've got this because God's got you.

Your new beginning can start right now if you're ready. Are you with me?

Moving Forward

Think about It

What scenario has you staring a new beginning in the face today? Is it a lifequake, a change of season, or simply a desire to start something fresh, new, and exciting?

Plan for It

What are the stumbling blocks—whether mental, emotional, or physical—that threaten to stand in the way of your quest to begin again? Make a list of those stumbling blocks on a piece of paper, and consider how they've kept you from moving forward. Then beside each one, jot down at least one idea for how you can overcome it and keep it from standing in the way of progress.

Act on It

Make a list of all the new things you want to begin. Write down at least three action items for each of those things, and set a deadline for when you want to accomplish each one. Dream big, but know that it's okay to start small. Every little step in the right direction is a positive step into your future. And remember, nothing is ever impossible unless we decide it is and give up.

Pray over It

Jesus, I invite You into this adventure with me today as I embark on my new beginning. I need Your strength and peace to pursue this new season of life and overcome all the challenges that lie ahead. Give me the wisdom to be aware of my emotions and the ability to control my thoughts so neither of them will become a hindrance. Pick me up when I stumble, but help me view every stumble as a learning experience that can push me forward. Fill me with excitement about this fresh start, about feeling joy again, and about trusting You all along the way to open the right doors and protect me and my heart. Amen.

Write your own prayer to Jesus in this space.

Chapter 2

How Did I Get Here?

How did I get here? And where exactly is *here*?

Unfortunately, I've had to ask myself this question many times over the years. Times when circumstances changed, one season faded into the next, the familiar became a memory, and unknowns tangled themselves in my heart and mind.

Here is the starting line where we're faced with leaving what we once knew as normal and we face the challenge of beginning again in one way or another. I have lots of examples to share with you, but I'll begin with a recent experience of beginning again.

Just over eight years ago as of the writing of this book, it felt as if the train of life I had been riding on slammed into a brick wall when my marriage of twenty-five years imploded because of circumstances beyond my control (if you're reading this and experiencing something similar, check out my book *Living Unbroken: Reclaiming Your Life and Your Heart after Divorce*, as well as *Living Unbroken: A Divorce Recovery Workbook*).

For years, I had asked God to mend and protect my marriage, but the reality is, as we all know, what we pray for isn't always what we get. Not because God didn't hear our prayers or care about our needs, desires, or pleas for compassion. In many places in the Bible, we're told He hears our prayers. For example, Jeremiah 29:12 says, "When you call on me, when you come and pray to me, I'll listen" (MSG).

Sometimes we don't get what we pray for because God's plans aren't our plans, yet His plans are always best. In fact, sometimes God takes us on a journey we didn't know we needed in order to bring us everything we didn't even know we wanted. We have to accept that life can turn out differently than we imagined and believe that He knows what is best for us and our future—even if we don't see the logic or like the outcome.

As a result of this lifequake, I became a single woman, single mother, and sole provider practically overnight. I found myself at a crossroads where every direction looked like it led to a cliff. A crossroads where I felt tied to a train track and unable to move, all the while sure that something even worse was going to roll down the tracks soon. Helpless. Hopeless. Directionless. I was wandering like a lost puppy in a season of hurt, confusion, and transitions I never wanted to be in.

After some therapy and a lot of prayer and determination, I realized I had become an enabler of my husband's unhealthy patterns of behavior. I had been accepting the unacceptable and forgiving the unforgivable, rather than following my instincts, trusting God, and building the confidence to take control of my life and future. The time came when I knew it was the right moment to move into the new phase God was pulling me toward, despite having no idea how I would survive. I had tried to hang on and keep my family together at all costs, including my own sanity and self-respect, but I finally found peace about letting go of the past, releasing what could no longer be, and choosing to embrace what could be with God's love, grace, protection, and provision.

The reason you're in a season of change and transition is likely very different than I've described, but regardless of our situation, God will make it clear to us when change is needed in any area of life. We just feel it in our spirits and can confirm it by listening for God's whispers. And when we receive that holy clarity, we also receive peace, courage, and confidence to do the hardest of things (in blind faith, I might add).

Sometimes God takes us on a journey we didn't know we needed in order to bring us everything we didn't even know we wanted.

Even though I barely knew how to handle all the circumstances of the present day, much less had the slightest inkling of how to press ahead, I knew it was time to make the transition to my new normal. I knew it was time to begin again. My heart longed to embrace the vision of better and happier times.

But still, can I be honest? I didn't want to begin again. I had no idea how to start over all alone after twenty-five years of marriage. I couldn't help but raise my fists in anger and hurt and express to God the deepest questions burning in my soul: *How—and, more importantly, why—did I get here? I don't like it one single bit! It's not fair! I don't want to start over, especially at this point in my life! I don't even know where to begin. I don't know how. Plus, I'm scared.*

One day as the words *starting over* rattled through my mind again, my knees buckled, and I crumpled to the floor like a pile of dirty laundry. Apparently those two words held more power over my soul than I had recognized before. The fear of starting over had not only caused me to overlook the opportunities tied to beginning again but had also been controlling every decision I'd made for years, including poor ones with negative impacts, and now I was forced to accept and face that fear head on.

But it wasn't easy. How can you begin again when you're lost in the obscurity of your ordinary days and a better future seems not only impossible to envision but also entirely out of reach?

Yet the time came when I had no choice but to accept the reality that *beginning again* was unavoidably my new story. And maybe in an entirely different way, you're realizing that for yourself too. Stick with me here—we're now in this together.

The next couple of years seemed to pass as slowly as molasses seeping out of a mason jar, with each day dripping with new sorrow or problems. Little by little, I made progress, got back on my feet, and transitioned into this wilderness as best I could. I had gotten into a new routine of living and thought I was making headway.

But then a day came that I had been dreading. It wasn't a bad day and happens to countless moms, but it was difficult nonetheless.

My older daughter had already graduated from college, and my middle child was in her final year, when the youngest of my three children—my baby boy, who had become my rock and my best friend, who kept me strong, who spent every day with me after school, and who had become the man of the house far too soon—was all grown up and moving off to college as well. It was another major adjustment shaking up my already-shattered existence, leaving another hole in my heart with the term *empty nester* settling deep into the gaping spaces. And to make matters worse, I was an empty nester all alone, dealing with the emotions of sending my last-born child out into the world.

The day I moved him into his freshman dorm, with the help of my two daughters, was filled with excitement for the new life he was embarking on. I held in my emotions all day, so as not to spoil the mood for everyone, but when I returned home alone to a painfully empty, quiet house? Lord, help us all.

Change was one thing. We all go through it from time to time. But in my mind, the amount of change I had been through over the span of just a few years was getting ridiculous. I had endured so many "lasts" in so many circumstances, and I was emotionally drained. I couldn't help but wonder what else was in store for me. All the uncertainties were so scary, and I was shaken.

I know I sound like a drama queen. It certainly wouldn't be the first time I've been accused of that! Claiming it. Owning it. But seriously, I bet all you empty-nester mamas out there can relate. I had been secretly dreading this day for months, feeling like it would surely be the death of me and my last shred of happiness. I had been hanging on to normalcy by a thread, and this was indeed the absolute end of what was left of my formerly semi-normal life. College dorm room all set up, last child out the door, mommy days officially over after twenty-four years of my children being my biggest priority.

Another rearrangement of life to face, accept, and learn to deal with, all alone and with no way of turning back or changing anything. I was so proud of my children for who they had become and all they were accomplishing, but still, it was hard on my heart to accept that time was moving on, they were moving on, and I needed to let go and move on too, whatever that meant.

As my son settled into his new dorm that evening, I sat on my bed staring into the dresser mirror, with the only noise being the low voices on the television. Who was that woman looking back at me? That woman who had no idea how to process what had happened to the life she once knew?

I saw a reflection of someone I didn't even recognize. Someone who didn't know who she was, much less who she was supposed to be or who she could become. A broken woman who didn't know how to begin again or where to even start.

I was 100 percent officially both feet into a new phase of life. Again. And again, I didn't like it.

What did I do next? At first I did what most people do.

I pouted. I felt depressed. I had lots of pity parties. I cried. I grieved. I isolated myself. I prayed and searched for meaning and purpose. I had bouts of anger. I made mistakes while trying to fill the emptiness and numb the pain. I longed for answers and grasped for direction. I let fear, worry, and loneliness become my closest companions.

But over time, I began to learn the true value of beginning again and discovered it was the best thing that had ever happened to me. And if you give me a chance, I want to help you realize it can be the best thing that has ever happened to you too. God is still writing your story.

Take Chances on New Changes

Gradually, I pulled myself up by my bootstraps and forced myself to be strong. I leaned heavily on my faith, consistently praying for clarity and guidance on what next steps I needed to take in every area of my life. I learned there are times when God uses our deepest pain to launch us on the path to our greatest callings and adventures. I had to forget what was gone, grow to appreciate what still remained, be thankful for the wisdom I had gained over the years, and look forward to what was coming next.

Due to the divorce and having no income to depend on, I had to get a full-time job for the first time in fifteen years. And after I had spent months searching to no avail, feeling like I had nothing to offer any organization anywhere, God opened the perfect door to the perfect job in His perfect timing. I also wrote a new book. In fact, four new books (*Unsinkable Faith, Love Life Again, Living Unbroken*, and *Living Unbroken: A Divorce Recovery Workbook*) over the next few years, none of which would have been written had I not been through such a difficult season of changes, hurt, and healing and witnessed how God can pull us up from the bottom of the deepest pit and set us on the firm foundation of new and wonderful beginnings.

I started playing tennis more. I learned how to play golf. I signed up for community social events so I could meet new people, make new friends, and get myself out of the house (yes, it was awkward and out of my comfort zone, but it was worth it!).

I scoured thrift and antique stores looking for inexpensive old pieces of furniture to refinish, because turning something old and lifeless into something new and beautiful always gives me a sense of pride and accomplishment. I took chances and began some other new things too, which I can't wait to tell you about through the pages of this book, especially since I could see God's fingerprints all over them in miraculous ways.

But the point is, I had to make a choice. Would I allow myself to stay stuck in the gloomy fog of transitions, refusing to give life another shot and mad about having to begin again? Or would I embrace where God had me, expect the best from Him, and make the most of the new season He had me in? Would I continue to believe the lie that joy and blessings were things of the past? Or would I allow myself to have hope that new blessings were on the horizon? Would I stay glued to the old and lifeless? Or would I take chances on the new changes God had in store?

Thankfully, I chose the latter of each of these. And you can too.

Embracing change is a choice we all face when transitions roll in like huge waves. We can view transitions with a pessimistic, disheartened, or angry attitude, or we can view them optimistically, with hope and trust that God has good plans for our future.

Zig Ziglar, well-known author and speaker, is credited with this insight: "You must make a choice to take a chance or your life will never change."

The day I realized and accepted that I was the only one who could change my life for the better and committed to take a chance at doing so, everything changed. No one else could do it for me, and although God could guide me, it was up to me to be brave and move ahead. I concluded that my happiness wasn't going to happen by chance; I had to make the choice to take action and make it happen for myself.

I've since come to realize that sometimes we must walk away from what we thought we wanted to find what makes us thrive and brings us joy. And more times than not, the bad things that happen in our lives—or even just those hard seasons of change—put us directly on the path to the best things that will ever happen to us. No matter who we are or what happens to us, we all have the chance to turn our lives around and make them great.

So I embarked on my journey, taking one step at a time, and every step led to the next. With each step, I got a little bit stronger and grew a little bit more.

And you know what? The new beginning awaiting me turned out to be awesome.

Moving Forward

Think about It

Is there an area of your life in which you need to accept that change is needed? Is it time to let go of the past and embrace your next phase in blind faith? What encouraging, motivating advice would you give a friend in your situation?

Plan for It

Write down the advice you would give that friend, and now send an email to yourself with that same advice. Would you encourage your friend to take a chance on renewed happiness? Then encourage yourself to do so too.

Act on It

On a piece of paper or in a Word document, draw or create three columns. Title the first column "Life Changes," the middle column "If I Stay Stuck," and the third column "If I Move Forward."

In the left-hand column, make a list of the changes that have happened in your life recently—the ones that have disrupted your normal and left you reeling with confusion about how to let go of the past, adjust to this new season, and step into your future.

In the center column, explain what your life will look like if you stay stuck in denial or depression and refuse to move forward or change. These are the negatives of not embracing beginning again.

And in the far-right column, write down what your life could look like if you let go of the past, accepted the current changes, and took a chance on starting anew. What might you do differently? What could you start doing that you've been putting off? What would be better? How would you feel? What are the positives that could be a part of your new beginning? What part of this new season is exciting to imagine?

How does seeing those benefits and opportunities in black and white motivate you to embrace the reality of your new beginning and take a chance on renewed happiness and contentment?

How would you feel if you gave your *new* the fighting chance it deserves?

Pray over It

Lord, I am sad that my life has changed so much, and I feel lost and directionless right now. I don't feel confident about stepping into the new, but I ask that You give me a boldness of faith to trust You and move forward into my new beginning. Help me focus on the positives and feel Your presence as You hold my hand and walk me through the fog into the beautiful future You have mapped out for me. Amen.

Write your own prayer to Jesus in this space.

Chapter 3

Keep Your Eyes on the Horizon

A transition is a beautiful season when God strips off what is old to welcome in the new, sort of like when I scrape the old paint chips off a worn-out dresser and freshen it up with a beautiful new color of paint. It's simply a process or a period of changing from one state or condition to an alternate one. Turning the old into something new and improved. A transition or season of change is merely a crossing from one place to another, essentially a bridge from one stage of life to the next. But these bridges can be tough to cross, especially when we don't know what is on the other side.

That is where that blind faith I mentioned comes into play. Leaving behind the known while not knowing what will be is like being trapped in a hallway between closed doors, desperately trying to figure out which one should be opened and wishing we knew where each led. Or a hallway of fun-house mirrors where anxiety and uncertainty cause us to feel warped and panicked with confusion.

It is faith alone that will help us exit one phase and move into the next season or opportunity with an attitude of joy and hopeful expectation.

With strength that can come only from God and with confidence and courage in tow. If we wait until we feel like we have solid ground beneath our feet and have it all figured out, we may miss the opportunities in front of us right now.

Or maybe you're not in a season of transition. Maybe nothing much has changed for you at all, except your contentment and happiness. And therein lies the problem.

You're tired of the mundane. Bored with where you are and frustrated with not knowing how to change it. You might *like* to experience a transition, but instead, life just keeps going down the familiar path, day in and day out. Same ol', same ol'. Even so, you feel stuck at a crossroads, longing for a new direction. Maybe you're longing for the unfamiliar, craving new adventures or opportunities, but you feel unsure you have what it takes to bring your dreams and ideas to fruition.

Every end is a new beginning if we give it a fighting chance. Although most of us don't enjoy going through change, even when it presents many advantages, change is often the best thing that can happen to us—or the best thing we can make happen.

During a conversation about overcoming mental stumbling blocks with well-known author and neuroscientist Dr. Caroline Leaf, Dr. Adi Jaffe, a nationally recognized expert on mental health, said, "It's not that you can't change.... You are constantly changing. [But] are you going to take charge of what that change is going to be? Are you going to dictate what the change is going to be, or are you going to just kind of let it happen haphazardly and allow the world to dictate what [the] change will be?"[1] I'd rather be in charge of my own life, destiny, and happiness. How about you?

We all have it in us to change and adapt, but we must be willing to trust that God always has a plan, even if it's not what we want or understand. If we're truly going to trust God's plans, we have to start by being willing to let go of what we think our lives are supposed to look like and be grateful for everything that is.

I'll be the first to admit that although I know I should trust God's plans wholeheartedly and believe He has my best interests at heart, it's not easy.

Every end is a new beginning if we give it a fighting chance.

One of the key verses I've always clung to is Jeremiah 29:11: "'I know the plans I have for you,' says the LORD. 'They are plans for good and not for disaster, to give you a future and a hope.'" That verse helped me hang on to hope during so many hopeless times. It gave me a shred of comfort even when life was as uncomfortable and unfamiliar as it could possibly get.

As I faced yet another trying season of changes after my divorce and tried to believe God had another good plan for me, I looked up that verse to soothe my soul. I wanted to see it in black and white as a stark reminder that it still existed. I wanted to believe His plans were still good, but I'm not going to lie—it was getting harder and harder by the day. It's normal for faith to waver when adversities are crushing our spirits, but if we look for God during our desperate moments, we will see Him.

As I researched Jeremiah 29:11 during this time, God opened my eyes in a new way, and I gained a whole new perspective, not only about my "life verse," as people often say, but about this concept of God's plans overall.

Although I'm a Jesus girl and a woman who has spent years trying to be a faithful servant, I confess I've never been a Bible scholar. And like many solid, Bible-believing Christians, I've accidentally and innocently taken verses out of context at times. Jeremiah 29:11 turned out to be one of them.

Jeremiah 29:11 is one of the most quoted verses in the Bible. Christians all over the world cling to the promise of God's good plans for us, just as I did, even wearing it on sweatshirts, drinking out of coffee mugs with it inscribed across the front, and hanging it on the walls of our homes. You may have done that too. And it's okay!

But when we're faced with hard transitions, it's the context of this verse that will truly give us the hope we need. We all long to apply this as a promise that God has a perfect and wonderful plan for us individually, despite our circumstances. Our human hearts want to see God's plans falling into place, and when we don't or when it seems to be taking forever, our faith can begin to waver and our attitude can fly south. This is why understanding the true underlying meaning of this verse is so important, and that requires looking at the whole story, not just the one popular verse that brings us comfort and hope.

You see, Jeremiah 29:11 isn't God's personal promise to us at all, assuring us that things will be easy and always work out just like we want them to.

Now before you swing into debate mode, let me explain! This verse is, instead, God's promise to His people that His plans are always good regardless of whether they personally experience them or not. It's a promise that propels God's people to think beyond themselves—their problems, their lives, their transitions, and their desires—and trust in His sovereignty no matter what.

I've applied this verse to little ol' me for many, many years in various seasons of transition or adversity. It's always been *my* promise, *my* hope, from *my* God, from *my* Bible—I've always believed that things will be okay and everything will work out perfectly for *me* because He promised His plans are good. For *me*.

However, I've come to realize this verse isn't about individuals; it's about God's sovereign plans for all His people. The Bible teaches selflessness, not a me-centered faith, making it obvious we really can't make this verse all about us.

Let's Dig a Little Deeper

If we look at the verses before Jeremiah 29:11, we see God talking to the nation of Israel through the prophet Jeremiah. His people, who were in captivity in Babylon, were being told not that God was going to fix all their problems and get them out of their period of captivity but that, amid their hard circumstances, they should keep the faith and trust in His ways and plans wholeheartedly.

The Israelites had been in Egypt for generations, but their population had become so numerous that Pharaoh began to fear their presence and worried they would one day rise together and turn against the Egyptians. So, gradually and with great power and manipulation, Pharaoh forced them to become his slaves. I can only assume every single person began asking themselves, *How in the world did I get here?*

Jeremiah 29 begins by telling us that "Jeremiah wrote a letter from Jerusalem to the elders, priests, prophets, and all the people who had been exiled to Babylon by King Nebuchadnezzar" (v. 1).

He immediately shared with them a basic principle we should all cling to when we're faced with hard times: make the best of it and trust that God has a plan. It was a universal command, not a promise to individuals. Jeremiah 29:4–7 says, "This is what the LORD of Heaven's Armies, the God of Israel, says to all the captives he has exiled to Babylon from Jerusalem: 'Build homes, and plan to stay. Plant gardens, and eat the food they produce. Marry and have children. Then find spouses for them so that you may have many grandchildren. Multiply! Do not dwindle away! And work for the peace and prosperity of the city where I sent you into exile. Pray to the LORD for it, for its welfare will determine your welfare.'"

To summarize, Jeremiah encouraged them to make the best of where they were, even though they didn't like it. Although they were in a season of change and hardship, he wanted them to enjoy life, give it their all, and do what they could to make life good for all those around them. Notice how verse 7 ends: "Pray for Babylon's well-being. If things go well for Babylon, things will go well for you" (MSG). He commanded them to pray and continue praying because those prayers would be heard and they mattered.

Let's pause for a minute and imagine a crowd of Israelites hearing the prophets or elders read the letter aloud as they stood wide eyed, shoulder to shoulder, sweating under the heat of the sun and desperate to glean any glimmer of hope from their suffering. They were once free, yet they had been thrust into captivity in enemy territory. They were in a chapter of life that none of us would want to experience. I can only imagine they listened

with bated breath to Jeremiah's words—anxiously and expectantly waiting to hear God's miraculous plans to save them right away.

But that wasn't what God did. In verses 8 and 9, He told His people
to beware of all the false prophets claiming He was going to release them
soon because the truth was, His plan didn't include their release for seventy more years. Verse 10 says, "This is what the LORD says: 'You will be
in Babylon for seventy years. But then I will come and do for you all the
good things I have promised, and I will bring you home again.'"

That wasn't the good news they were hoping for. I mean seriously,
what kind of plan was that? Seventy more years in captivity? A wave of
disappointment must have raged through the hearts of the Israelites like
a tsunami. Not only would there be no immediate end to their suffering, but many of them wouldn't even live to see the days of freedom. The
common thread of thought was surely utter hopelessness, confusion, and
anger, tangled up with the temptation to lose faith altogether.

And this is where the popular verse comes into play: "'I know the
plans I have for you,' says the LORD. 'They are plans for good and not for
disaster, to give you a future and a hope'" (v. 11).

God told them they'd remain in captivity for quite some time. That
couldn't have been easy news to hear. I can almost hear the gasps and
moans that must have rippled through the crowd. I can't help but envision
His people falling to their knees, with wails of sorrow and fear splitting
the thick air. *But we don't like this! We don't want to be here! We did nothing to deserve this! Rescue us, Lord! Why are You waiting to change our lives
for the better? Do it now!* But His message didn't stop there.

Jeremiah 29:12–14 then says, "'In those days when you pray, I will
listen. If you look for me wholeheartedly, you will find me. I will be found
by you,' says the LORD." Again, prayer matters, and our prayers are heard.

Now that *is* the personal promise we can all take to heart, and surely it pricked even the rawest places in the souls of the Israelites. Despite their situation and despite the fact they were suffering and craved their freedom, they could find solace in the promise that if they continued to trust God and pray for their deepest desires, they would feel His presence and He would always be there with them and working for them, even if they couldn't see or understand what He was up to.

Then He left them with hope in verse 14: "I will end your captivity and restore your fortunes. I will gather you out of the nations where I sent you and will bring you home again to your own land." His promise of rescue and restoration wasn't spoken to an individual person. He didn't say He had a specific plan for every person in that crowd, lay out a blueprint of those plans, and promise that everyone would prosper immediately and live happily ever after.

Instead, He spoke of the bigger picture. His sovereign plans for all His people. Plans that were good in various ways for generations to come. He wanted to reassure them that even though their current situation was dire and things looked bleak, He was still in control and He had big plans. Therefore, they could be at peace and enjoy life right where they were, if they chose to.

This passage was intended to give hope to a group of people who were struggling with understanding what God was up to during a long, hard transition season. He wasn't going to change their circumstances right away, but He wanted them to change their hearts and minds.

And that's where you and I can relate most. When we struggle to understand what God is doing or we feel discouraged about our situation, we can make a conscious choice to make the most of the season we're in and trust that God is up to something good.

God's Plans Are Always Good

Although Jeremiah 29:11 was written *for* each of us, not *to* each of us, it's still a powerful reminder that God is always with us and He always has a plan for our good.

Even when life is hard, even when we feel like captives in a season we want to escape, even when the wait is painful, even when it seems life as we know it is falling apart around us ... God still has good plans for us. He sees us and hears our prayers. Mine and yours.

I've pleaded for God to rescue me from so many uncomfortable seasons. Although I was never in physical captivity like the Israelites, the stuckness, hopelessness, and desperation for change felt much the same. I was caught somewhere I didn't want to be with no hope of or belief in better times. The mounds of changes in front of me felt like fifty-foot walls I couldn't possibly climb over.

But hindsight is twenty-twenty. As I look back now, I can see God's presence and intervention through every stage of transition—the ones I enjoyed and the ones I endured. I can see how He was at work in the most painful of seasons in which I cried out for change that wasn't happening, even though at the time I was blind to what He was doing in the invisible realms. Just when I thought He was taking care of everyone else's problems but not mine, He was quietly leaving His fingerprints on every aspect of my life.

I can see now how, although I didn't understand my suffering, His plans were indeed good. For my benefit and the benefit of many others.

I take heart in realizing that no matter how bad things were, I found peace in Him in even the least peaceful circumstances and I lived with happiness in my heart even during hard times, only because He filled me with a joy that was undeniably from Him alone.

It was His hope that led me through many dark and difficult in-between stages of life, and His hope is what will lead you too. When you've been broken in any way, you can come out more beautiful than you ever were before, and although something might be gone, something better is always waiting ahead.

Should we still cling to Jeremiah 29:11? Absolutely! It serves as a reminder that although we face more difficulties and crossroads than we may ever want to experience, God's promises for His people are still true. He is faithful and He will never leave us.

In the context of this passage, God's people are the Israelites as a whole. But when Jesus died on the cross for our sins, He opened the door for everyone to be His people. We all belong to Him now. You and me. We are His children. His beloveds. His treasures. Thus, the foundational truth of this verse still applies to our lives today.

You see, in this passage, God was essentially telling the Israelites, *I see you. I know things are hard. I know you are hurting and losing hope. You think I don't hear your pleas? I know you are desperate for change. I see your period of transition. But ... live your life, get married, love and be loved, create generations, build legacies, work, play, thrive—right where I have you. Why? Because I promise, you've got this because I've got you. Things will get better in due time. A new beginning is on the horizon.*

My prayer is that digging into the true context of this passage hasn't brought you disappointment or discouragement or made you want to toss out your Jeremiah 29:11 coffee mug. Rather, I pray it has helped you form a new perspective about who you are in Christ. I hope it has ignited a fresh fire in your heart as you better understand that, throughout our troubles and difficult seasons, God does see us, He knows, He cares, He has our best interests in mind, and it's His desire that we learn to enjoy life right where we are while trusting Him with what lies ahead.

Once you decide this isn't where you want to be anymore or this isn't how you want to feel anymore, rest assured, you will find the inner desire to finally open the door for change. And in time, the day will come when you'll be able to say, "I may not be exactly where I want to be yet, but I thank God I'm not where I used to be." Isn't it exciting to think about being able to say that?

We don't have to like where God has us right now or like the ever-evolving stages of newness where we often find ourselves. But you know what? That's life for you. However, we can trust He has a plan and trust it is good, even when it doesn't make sense. We can live with unshakable certainty that He can see things we can't, and we can put all our faith into believing He is orchestrating a story we're not yet privy to.

Only then will we find the strength and willpower to accept where we are, tap into our inner tenacity and bravery, and truly embrace the blessing and adventure of beginning again.

Keep your eyes on the horizon, expectantly waiting for a glimpse of God's plan. One glimpse is all it will take to get you more excited about the *new* than you ever thought you could be. Yet while waiting on that glimpse, cling to the truth that God is ever present and He has good plans for you.

There's about to be a shift in your life. Get ready for it and the blessings it will bring.

Moving Forward

Think about It

What prayers has God not answered in the way you wanted Him to? What emotions did you experience because of feeling unseen and unheard by God?

Have you ever talked to God about those feelings and asked Him to give you peace even when you don't understand what He's up to? How does reminding yourself God really is listening make your heart feel lighter, even if just a little bit?

Plan for It

Make a list of all the changes that have happened in your life over the past six months, one year, or longer (or look back at the list you made under "Act on It" in chapter 2).

Write down all emotions you've experienced as a result. This gives you a true picture of not only your physical stumbling blocks but your mental ones as well so you can be prepared to tackle those obstacles head on in the future. Knowing what you need to change about yourself is crucial as you embark on new beginnings.

Act on It

Jot down the prayers that you feel God hasn't answered yet. Be honest with yourself and with God. Brainstorm some ideas for how you can continue to trust Him during periods of waiting to see Him at work.

During the wait for answered prayers and a glimpse of that story God is writing for your life, don't just sit idly by. Start taking some action! What can you do differently right now, today, to begin living life to the fullest just as God told the Israelites to do while they waited in captivity? Need a change of attitude or perspective? Start the transformation process by thinking about how you're thinking about things. You may have no control over some circumstances, but there are things you do have the power to change! Determine what those things are, and create a strategy for getting started.

Pray over It

Dear Jesus, forgive me for allowing disappointment about Your seeming lack of action to keep me from enjoying the blessings and opportunities I do have. Help me overcome fears, learn to have peace during the times of silence, and trust that You do have a great plan for me. Infuse me with the fortitude to start taking control of my thoughts and my actions. I commit to make some changes and take some steps forward, beginning today. Amen.

Write your own prayer to Jesus in this space.

Chapter 4

The Power of a Thought

The first holiday season after my husband moved out was one of the hardest I had ever experienced. I sat on the couch on Christmas Eve trying to hold back my tears as my three children, two in their teens and one in college, stood in front of me holding Christmas presents in their arms, which I had wrapped for them, while concerned and worried expressions covered their faces.

They were headed to their paternal grandmother's house for Christmas dinner, just as we had done for more than twenty years, but this year was different. For the first time in their entire lives, they were going to our annual family holiday gathering without me.

I knew this was hard on them too, as it had been only a couple of months since all our lives were turned upside down and our hearts broken. So I put on a fake smile, assured them I would be fine, and encouraged them to have a nice visit. But inside, my heart was aching with a pain deeper than they would ever understand. Deeper than I could even understand myself. It felt as if my throat was closing as knots churned in my stomach. Not only did I feel broken, but my family felt broken, Christmas felt broken, and my life felt irreparably broken as well. Everything had changed, and nothing was the same. Including me.

After I watched the bright red taillights of their car disappear down the dark street, a deep sense of loneliness hung heavy in the air, drowning out the fresh pine scent of the tree. As I stared at the twinkling lights, the tears I had been holding back dripped down my cheeks. I didn't want to be in this unfamiliar space, this painful season of being separated from the most important people in my world—especially on my very favorite night of the year. Unable to join my extended family as I had done my entire adult life, I was forced to not only deal with the ache of loneliness but also face and accept the reality that they weren't even my family anymore and never would be again.

I knew things would evolve in time and circumstances would eventually get easier, but this particular juncture of beginning again—stuck painfully between the life I knew and an unknown future—was my biggest nightmare.

After a few minutes of sitting in my sadness and watching the flames dance in the fireplace through blurry, tear-filled eyes, I breathed out a heavy sigh, dried my face, and sat up straight. The only solace I could find was whispering to myself over and over the truth of God's promises in Scripture to always be with me, and even though my husband had left, my heavenly Father never would. As I sat in my den achingly alone on Christmas Eve, I began to feel the presence of Jesus right beside me, sweetly reminding me I wasn't alone after all.

I needed to refocus on the fact that even though my circumstances had changed and I literally hated my current season of massive adjustments, God was still the same sovereign God. His promise of peace, hope, and joy was still as valid as it ever was. I could have confidence that I would make it through and one day my life would be okay, possibly even better, and so would I.

That night, as my spirits lifted and I dug deep down inside myself to find the strength I was sure was in me, my mantra became "I've got this because God's got me." And I can't tell you how many times I had to repeat those words whenever my fears threatened to rise and my hope started to fall. This mantra became like a little pep talk I would give myself each time I felt my endurance and faith slipping, reminding myself I was a strong, smart, capable woman. I was strong in Christ, and Christ had all the strength I needed, just as we're told in 2 Corinthians 12:9: "My grace is all you need. My power works best in weakness." I had God, and He had me, and the more I held on to that truth, the more my outlook began to change.

Choose to Change and Grow

In Psalm 16, we read about a time when David felt weak, tired, alone, and lost, and he likely had to adopt a similar mantra. He was feeling especially left behind, forgotten, and afraid. Not only had life changed dramatically, but he was also hiding in the wilderness, possibly cowering under a bush or rock, hoping to go unseen while knowing Saul and his army were in hot pursuit to find him and kill him. Yet instead of letting his emotions shake him up, David shifted his attitude and chose to capture his thoughts and refocus on God's presence, which is exactly what I had to do that difficult Christmas Eve and every single day in the years since.

We see evidence of this in verse 8 when David said, "I know the LORD is always with me. I will not be shaken, for he is right beside me."

We can make the same choice David made when we're enduring hard times and new beginnings we never wanted. We can make new choices during those seasons when we wish we too could hide under a rock or bush and avoid the hard, unnerving circumstances that lurk in the territory of unknowns. We all experience countless situations that can make us feel alone, afraid, and abandoned, with no idea how we're going to get through and survive them, much less thrive on the other side.

Yet we too can remind ourselves God will never leave us or forsake us, so we can shift our minds and look Him in the face instead of cowering to our fears. When we keep our focus on His presence, our hearts are better equipped to handle anything life throws at us, especially during opportunities to begin again with no clue what the future holds. Why? Because we're never in this thing called life all alone.

I once read this quote: "Life is change; growth is optional. Choose wisely."[1] This speaks so much truth. Life will forever be changing. In fact, the only thing we can be assured of is that life will change. Which means we're always faced with the choice of letting change sink us or letting it catapult us into the new life God has in store.

But when everything around us seems to be changing, we often grasp for anything that will make us feel like the ground isn't shifting beneath our feet. Yet what we need most in order to find the security and hope we desperately long for is to focus on the scriptural truth that although life changes, God doesn't and He never will. God is unchanging, even in the midst of change.

Hebrews 13:8 reassures us of this truth: "Jesus Christ is the same yesterday, today, and forever." So does Malachi 3:6: "I am the LORD, and I do not change."

Let's face it. Even though as believers we know this to be true, in our hearts all those hope-stealing questions remain: Where is God right now when I need Him? Why isn't He answering my prayers? How will I make it through this? What if I feel I simply can't be who I want to be because the old me is still too raw? Even when we believe God doesn't change, our lives have changed and therefore we've changed, which makes the future feel even more blurry and scary at times.

No matter what I'm facing, I now understand that time and faith will always get me through and help me find myself in that new place—on the other side of transition—that I thought was beyond my grasp. And I feel sure I have plenty more opportunities to put that truth into practice!

For example, seven years after that first Christmas without my children, after I had finally settled into my single-mom, empty-nester life, I found myself facing yet another huge change.

I hesitantly made the hard but necessary choice to sell my family home, where my children and I had lived for twenty-five years, and purchase a smaller home. I knew it was time to move on, and the housing market was hot, so logically speaking, the timing was perfect. But, oh my goodness, it was hard on this girl's heart.

For weeks during the packing process, I fought the temptation to allow myself to dwell on thoughts that ushered in sadness rather than joy. Thoughts of the precious days of bringing my babies home from the hospital to that house and laying them in their freshly painted nurseries for the first time. Thoughts of how years later those rooms became colorful teenage-themed rooms (multiple times!). Memories of hosting birthday parties, cheerleading team gatherings, and football team sleepovers that ended with some scolding about ding-dong ditching houses in the neighborhood.

Recollections of hunting Easter eggs in the yard, shooting basketball in the driveway, playing in the playhouse in the woods out back, enjoying family cookouts, and grilling chicken wings while listening to Jimmy Buffett songs flooded my thoughts. Memories of the days when every nook and cranny of the house was filled with boxes of clothes, linens, and kitchen items as young adults packed up to leave for college and live on their own. Memories of when my family was in a better place. When life seemed normal and familiar. Stable and predictable yet not without its own set of problems, of course.

The stress of packing in the thick of all these reflections, coupled with an onslaught of accompanying emotions, felt overwhelming.

Moving day finally came, and it was rough. When I returned home from closing on my new house to continue loading my belongings into the moving truck, the new family had already shown up with their own trucks full of items for their new home. They had pushed my items aside and replaced them with their own. This wasn't supposed to happen, but some kind of error had occurred between attorneys in communication and timing, so unfortunately, it did.

Watching these strangers unload their things into *my* house was traumatizing, to say the least. It was chaotic and uncomfortable and rushed. I felt sad and angry and annoyed, all at the same time. I left some important belongings in the home simply because I couldn't manage to focus amid the chaos and stress long enough to make sure I had everything out.

I almost felt like I was an intruder in my own home, which escorted me straight into a full-blown emotional breakdown at the end of my driveway. When my sweet neighbors, who I had lived next door to from day one, came over to say their last goodbyes, I couldn't hold back the tears any longer as they hugged me and wished me the best. I finally got in my car and pulled out of *my* driveway for the very last time.

It may sound dramatic, but I felt numb. Confused. Lost. Paralyzed by all the feels that come with embarking on a new season and letting go of what once was. Change is hard.

When my former husband and I built that house decades earlier, my plan had been to retire there together and live happily ever after. I had envisioned precious grandkids toddling around on the same floors where my own children's little feet used to tread. I had dreamed of recreating with those babies all the special moments that I had enjoyed with my own kids. That was my plan.

That clearly wasn't God's plan, and it was a hard pill to swallow. Yet God had allowed this change in my life to occur, and He blessed me with a beautiful new house I never dreamed I would be able to obtain on my own. So, despite feeling a little displaced and needing time to feel at home in my new house, I let joy seep in, focusing on more evidence of God's hand at work behind the scenes for all the years prior. I chose to embrace this new beginning with everything I had.

As hard as it was, the chaos of the new owners unexpectedly arriving before they were supposed to was possibly, in hindsight, a little blessing in disguise. It forced me to face the reality, even if abruptly, that that house was no longer *my* home. It now belonged to someone else. A new family was embracing their new beginning in their new home, and I had to embrace my new beginning as well.

A few months after I moved, two of my children got married only two months apart. It was a season of flurry, stress, planning, and joy that led to two of the sweetest, most beautiful weddings I've ever attended (I'm not biased, of course). And although their weddings were unforgettable, immense blessings and I will forever be grateful for the amazing, Jesus-loving spouses God brought into my children's lives, it meant even more changes for me as a single mom and especially for our future family holidays and traditions.

A few months later in early December, as I was spending my first Christmas season in my wonderful new home, I found myself pondering how much life had changed, secretly mourning the way things used to be, even though the past certainly wasn't perfect. Not knowing if my children and their spouses would make it home for the holidays, I was slowly slipping into discouragement and cursing change under my breath. Why couldn't some things in life stay the same?

In that very moment, I was struck with a sobering thought: *We have a choice which rooms in our minds we allow ourselves to walk into, Tracie. The rooms where we let our thoughts linger will always determine our joy.*

The thought took me aback. Where had it come from, right in the middle of the pity party I was gladly throwing for myself? It was a gentle whisper from God, telling me to pick my head up, shift my thoughts, and focus on all the good things He had done for me during all the transitions in my life, including this one. It was a reminder that although this season of change was difficult, this too would pass and I would be okay. Just like eight years earlier when my thoughts were rampant with negativity, God needed to reel me back in yet again.

You see, our minds are filled with rooms of memories. Some rooms we'd prefer not to visit, yet we wander right into them. Rooms filled with memories of grief, heartbreak, and loss. Rooms filled with seasons gone by and days we wish we could get back or do over. Rooms filled with memories that look much different from the present. Rooms filled with unfulfilled desires, unmet expectations, or loneliness.

But there are also those rooms where we love to let our minds linger. Rooms that hold all those fond memories of special times. Rooms filled with thoughts of beloved family and friends, God-ordained blessings, hope, and so much more.

I had to switch directions in my mind and choose which rooms my thoughts would visit most during this period of adaptation.

That one small decision was a game changer.

Capture Every Thought

The Bible talks repeatedly about how powerful our thoughts are. For example, Proverbs 4:23 says, "Be careful what you think, because your thoughts run your life" (NCV). If our thoughts are negative, our hearts will be too, which in turn affects how we live our lives. Proof of this can be found in Proverbs 17:22, which says, "A cheerful heart is good medicine, but a crushed spirit dries up the bones" (NIV). How we think impacts how we feel and live, and who wants a heart void of cheer? Who wants to feel like their spirit is crushed? Who wants to be bone tired? Who longs to feel sad and depressed and stuck in the past all the time? Who wants to mourn what they don't have instead of fully embracing and enjoying all the blessings they do have?

Certainly not me! And I feel confident you don't either. Instead, we can choose positive thoughts that will always steer us toward those rooms in our minds that bring us joy. I also love this quote from popular author and Bible teacher Joyce Meyer, which makes this point even clearer: "Being negative only makes a difficult journey more difficult. You may be given a cactus, but you don't have to sit on it."[2] Truth! Optimism is a choice, and it's ours to make, no matter how many cacti we receive in the throes of life.

Romans 12:2 says, "Don't copy the behavior and customs of this world, but let God transform you into a new person by changing the way you think." If we acknowledge that our thoughts are standing in the way of our happiness and ability to change, and if we are ready and willing to shift our thought patterns, then God is ready and willing to help us change.

Each morning after God reminded me of this powerful truth and prompted me to reclaim control over my thoughts, I arose from my bed and saw the twinkling lights of the Christmas tree, but instead of feeling sadness, I began to mentally run into those rooms filled with beautiful memories, gratitude, and blessings. I opened the doors to see the beauty God has allowed me to enjoy in each season, which helped me shift my focus from what is no longer to all the blessings in the present and those to come.

> You and I can achieve the impossible through Christ and through our decision to change ourselves, our thoughts, and our paths. Choose to see the good, not the bad.

You can do the same today! Slam shut the doors to all those rooms that threaten to steal your joy, and commit to keeping your thoughts from creeping into them. Ask God to capture each thought that tries to pull you back into sadness, disappointment, fear, or confusion, and run into the rooms full of joyful and happy thoughts. Don't visit the rooms filled with insecurities, fears, and apprehensions, and instead, direct your mind into the rooms full of hope and excitement for what is to come.

No matter what type of transition you're facing right now, your thoughts will determine how you feel and ultimately how you live. Every time we're faced with navigating a realignment of life, our thoughts will be the foundation for our growth or the lack thereof.

Ponder this well-said adage: "The positive thinker sees the invisible, feels the intangible, and achieves the impossible." You and I can achieve the impossible through Christ and through our decision to change ourselves, our thoughts, and our paths. Choose to see the good, not the bad.

We can all learn how to be happy with what we have while we pursue all we want. We don't always need a new day to start over, because sometimes we only need a new mindset.

It takes intentionality to focus on our blessings instead of our burdens and embrace what God has for us each day with open minds and hearts full of faith, but it will always change our lives for the better.

Moving Forward

Think about It

How are you feeling with regard to what once was and what is yet
to be? What thoughts do your memories evoke? Are your thoughts
feeding optimism and happiness? Or are they instead feeding
negativity and sadness? Your mind will always believe what you
tell it. What are you telling it?

Plan for It

When things change inside you, things will change around you. Think of the ways you may be growing from your experience or season of transition. What are some ways you can begin capturing your negative thoughts and shifting those patterns to be more hopeful and joyful?

Act on It

Write out a commitment to yourself to transform your thought habits, move forward, thrive, and grow; then jot down any areas you already know you'd like to grow in.

Write Hebrews 13:8 ("Jesus Christ is the same yesterday, today, and forever") and Malachi 3:6 ("I am the LORD, and I do not change") on a sticky note or piece of notebook paper. Post it on your refrigerator or your bathroom mirror to remind yourself each day that although life is changing, God is not.

Put your smile on! Wear it everywhere you go, every day. Starting today. Think positive, be positive, and live positive.

Pray over It

Lord, help me be acutely aware of what mental rooms my thoughts are visiting, and slam shut the doors to those rooms that will steal my joy. Help me capture my thoughts and stay focused on You and the many blessings in my life. Fill me with peace amid change and chaos, and infuse me with a sense of hopefulness and joyfulness that I can find only in You. Amen.

Write your own prayer to Jesus in this space.

Chapter 5

Understanding Transitions and Mistakes to Avoid

Transitions are never easy, whether they are happening because of circumstances beyond our control or because of a change we hoped would happen. But having a better understanding of transitions, coupled with our continued faith in God, will empower us to come out on the other side. And when I say "us," I mean you, my friend.

I bet you can relate to facing a lifequake and having to accept the reality of the losses that came along with it. The painful awareness of the old things, people, blessings, and feelings you had to leave behind. The fear of the unknown as you investigate the blank space in your future, which you don't know how to fill. A new path can seem scary, even if the old path was laced with hardships of its own.

The word *transition* can be defined as "movement, passage, or change from one position, state, stage, subject, concept, etc., to another; change."[1]

As I said before, change can be hard to welcome, especially when we didn't want that change to occur. But if we embrace it and allow God to lead us through it, it can turn out to be a blessing and we can learn and grow in ways we would have never expected.

Successfully moving through your journey depends on knowing what kind of transition, or new beginning, you're currently facing.

One researcher has identified four types of life transitions: anticipated, unanticipated, nonevent, and sleeper transitions.[2] Each one brings its own set of challenges and opportunities for growth, but understanding which type of transition we're going through can give us the strength and tools to get through the process.

Let's take a moment to define these four types of transitions so you can begin thinking about where you are today.

Anticipated Transitions

Anticipated transitions are those you expected to happen, whether you wanted them to or didn't want them to, and even those you intentionally made happen. Getting married is a transition you wanted to happen, but it can still be hard in the early stages, as it's a huge adjustment. Having a baby is something you anticipate and one of the biggest transitions a woman can go through. Although becoming a mom for the first time isn't always easy, in time you figure out your way and thank God for the little baby you hold in your arms. If you decide to go back to college, move to a new house or a new state, change your career, or end a relationship, these are decisions you made for yourself. However, when these transitions occur as you expected, they may feel harder than you imagined.

My friend Michelle shared with me about a time she made some changes that ended up being tougher than she thought they'd be. She switched churches and jobs at the same time after a relationship breakup. She also ended up losing a few friends, switching to a new gym, and saying goodbye to her best friend when that friend moved hours away. All these changes happened within a short period of time, and she felt overwhelmed, alone, and confused in this unfamiliar season, even though she had ushered several of those changes into her life on purpose. But Michelle focused on keeping routines, praying, and looking for God at work. She committed to studying the Bible, finding new friends, seeing a Christian therapist, and finding creative outlets to channel her energy.

Michelle smiles now when she talks about how much she grew in listening to God's voice, following His lead, and embracing her opportunity for new beginnings, even though it wasn't easy. She started a successful small business and grew as a women's ministry leader. She began writing a Bible study, which led her to self-publish her own book. She also is thankful for the community she started building for herself, which has become her family, and she can clearly see how God used her hard transitions for so much good.

Over a few short years, Cathy moved to a new country, got married, had a baby, and became a stay-at-home mom, all of which were planned and anticipated yet still difficult transitions to make, especially at the same time. Unfortunately, she later went through a divorce, which left her nearly homeless due to having no job, no money, and no family in that country to help her. Even though her life was crumbling and she was facing many unknowns, she knew she needed to stay strong for her daughter. So she stood firm in her faith, grounded herself in prayer, practiced meditation, and immersed herself in a small circle of amazing, supportive women.

In time, Cathy landed a great job and was able to get her first apartment on her own. She was eventually able to purchase her own home, which gave her enough capital to buy her own business and launch a brand-new career. Her faith in God's plans for her future was renewed, and she has no doubt He knows what is best for her.

Whatever the anticipated event, it typically feels uncomfortable, overwhelming, and stressful at first. We may doubt why we wanted that change in the first place, and we may even begin to regret our choices if things don't go as planned. We can all get to a point where we doubt and question ourselves. *What was I thinking? Why didn't God give me a warning or guide me better?* But we can trust that things will turn out okay, because God's got us and we have Him.

Unanticipated Transitions

Unanticipated transitions are those situations you didn't plan for. Circumstances you never envisioned as part of your story. For example, hearing your husband say he doesn't love you anymore or finding out he's found someone else, receiving a scary diagnosis, enduring the unexpected death of a loved one, losing a job, or getting involved in an accident. These are times when life jumps the train track and you feel out of control, lost in your body and in your life, with stress and fear running rampant in your heart and mind. But God's arms are always around you.

My friend Cheryl experienced an unanticipated transition twenty years ago when she left a job she loved but not by choice. She struggled with feeling like a failure, losing her identity, and facing a very uncertain future. But she brushed herself off and started a Bible study with a few trusted ladies, and that study is still going strong today with lots of new faces. God opened a door for her when she needed it most, and then after six months without a job, she landed one that ended up being the most fulfilling, soul-stretching, and challenging position she had ever held. She recently retired from that job, and she thanks God for leading her through that season and for the experiences she was able to have as a result.

Gerolene lost her husband of forty years unexpectedly in 2021. Just before he passed, the Lord had laid 1 Peter 5:10 on her heart: "In his kindness God called you to share in his eternal glory by means of Christ Jesus. So after you have suffered a little while, he will restore, support, and strengthen you, and he will place you on a firm foundation." Gerolene knew that the Lord was calling her husband home and that He would give her strength to get through it. Next she was prompted to read Romans 8:11: "The Spirit of God, who raised Jesus from the dead, lives in you. And just as God raised Christ Jesus from the dead, he will give life to your mortal bodies by this same Spirit living within you." She didn't fully connect with the meaning of this verse until later in her healing journey, but within a few months, she realized losing her husband had caused her to grow closer to God. He had also impressed Hebrews 13:5 on her spirit: "Never will I leave you; never will I forsake you" (NIV). And He stayed true to that promise.

She expressed how she had never known the severity of pain from losing a spouse and even thought about wanting to die herself after having lost the love of her life. The gaping hole in her heart felt unmendable, and she thought she would never heal. But God was with her constantly, reminding her He was preparing her to meet Him one day too.

Gerolene said, "Had God not taken my husband, I would not have grown so much spiritually. I would not have searched His Word as I did and still do. I know without a doubt that I will see my beloved again and God kept me here to grow me for a higher purpose."

God knew what Cheryl and Gerolene were going through, and they can now both see in retrospect that although they didn't understand His plans and their hearts were broken, He had a good plan, He knew what He was doing, He had them in His grasp, and He never left their side.

Nonevent Transitions

Nonevent transitions are times when you anticipated a change but it doesn't happen or it doesn't happen how you wanted it to. Maybe you had hoped for a promotion at work, but a less qualified person received that promotion instead. Maybe you thought you were pregnant, but test results proved otherwise. Maybe you thought your new church was exactly where you were supposed to be, but certain interactions with congregation members made you doubt that. Maybe you thought you would be in a different place at this stage of your life, and the reality of where you are is disheartening. These types of situations can usher in grief and a feeling of loss, even though nothing severely traumatic occurred. But God's arms are always around you.

I met a lady named Amy who experienced this type of transition when she was passed over for the CEO position after a merger took place at the nonprofit she had worked at for thirty-two years. She was devastated and left that organization. She felt confused about why God had allowed the ending of the long-term career she had worked so hard at, rendering her clueless about what her new beginning would look like, much less how she would fill the open spaces during such an unfamiliar adjustment period.

Within a year, Amy had a new grandson, who she was able to care for anytime, and her parents moved closer to where she lived. Shortly after, both of her parents got sick, and since she wasn't working, she had the precious gift of time to take care of them before they passed away within two weeks of each other. Amy shared that although she didn't understand what God was up to when she became unemployed, He knew she would need free time to serve her family, and she is now so thankful. Amy said, "I had a plan, but God had a better plan. I am thankful for a deep-rooted faith that helped me believe when I didn't understand." Amy had God on her side, and in the midst of the transition, He was blessing her with the time she needed. He had her and her life in His hands, and He knew what was best.

Sleeper Transitions

Sleeper transitions are the ones that occur without much thought around them. One day you realize you're great at your job because you've gradually improved your competence through training and personal development. Maybe a meaningful parenting encounter happens, and you recognize you're doing a pretty good job of raising the children God gave you after all.

Perhaps you travel overseas and can use that second language you've been practicing, and you find that you can communicate well in any scenario. Or you win a 5K race and see the fruits of all the energy and effort you put into training for it even though you had doubts about whether or not you could finish. Maybe you felt led to write a book but thought it was impossible, and after days of pouring your thoughts onto paper, you suddenly see your manuscript taking shape.

Sleeper transitions can also be negative, like when a friendship or relationship slips away and one day you become conscious of the fact you haven't been communicating with that person for quite some time. Or when driving to work, you feel a strange sense of dread or boredom bubbling up in your spirit, which is alarming because you always felt you liked your job. You look at your children and notice how big they've grown and wonder how it happened so quickly yet right before your eyes. Possibly you wake up before daylight and suddenly feel acutely aware of the years that have passed and the time you've wasted not pursuing your deepest dreams.

Sleeper transitions take you by surprise when your eyes are opened to see what has happened, and they can bring on confusion, concern, or regret. But again, God's arms are always around you.

Each type of transition is unique, but the underlying emotions can be the same. No season of change is worry- or problem-free. But when we trust God's arms are always around us—to hold us up when we're weak and catch us when we fall—all the while believing He has a good plan for our lives even if we can't see it yet, we can keep running the race and trusting that God is paving the way.

The best gift we can ever give ourselves is to learn how to transition well, no matter what. And that involves learning how to cross over from where we were, to where we are, to where we long to be.

Mistakes to Avoid

Before we can focus on how to begin embracing the new, it's important to recognize the stumbling blocks that may trip us up so that we can avoid them.

The first mistake we can make that will keep us from moving into the next stage of life with confidence is exactly what I did during the holidays a few years ago. Instead of focusing on all my current blessings and looking forward, I was looking back. In fact, for years, I was the poster child for looking back, mourning all that had been lost in the aftermath of my divorce. Consumed with wishing things were different while having no power to change them. Reliving all the sweet memories of the past, to the point where they crippled my present-day happiness and blinded me to everything I had to be thankful for.

When we're looking back, we can't look forward. Either we're looking in the rearview mirror of life, or we're looking at the road ahead. Have you ever tried to drive your car in reverse for more than a block? It's not nearly as effective as driving forward. So, if we want to transition well, looking forward is the key to success. It will always work in our favor to accept what is, let go of what was, and have faith in what will be.

The apostle Paul is a great example of doing this. In Philippians 3, he shared a message about the value of knowing Christ. He reminded the people of Philippi that nothing mattered more than having a relationship with their Savior, and he shared tips for how they could prioritize Him daily. Then he gave them encouragement to keep pushing forward.

Paul wrote, "I don't mean to say that I have already achieved these things or that I have already reached perfection. But I press on to possess that perfection for which Christ Jesus first possessed me. No, dear brothers and sisters, I have not achieved it, but I focus on this one thing: Forgetting the past and looking forward to what lies ahead, I press on to reach the end of the race and receive the heavenly prize for which God, through Christ Jesus, is calling us" (vv. 12–14).

Take note of verse 13, where Paul encouraged them to forget the past and look forward to what was ahead. He wanted them to leave the past behind and trust that God had already gone ahead of them and planned the way. Deuteronomy 31:8 also assures us of this truth: "Do not be afraid or discouraged, for the LORD will personally go ahead of you. He will be with you; he will neither fail you nor abandon you."

We can all look back from time to time and remember the good seasons we've cherished. Our memories will always be in our minds, the sweet ones and the bitter ones. We can learn from the past and rely on that wisdom, but we can't live in the past because it is, well, in the past.

We can only walk into our new season, living one day at a time and focusing on what God is doing right now.

The second mistake we can make is letting fear take root in our hearts during our hard seasons. It's totally normal and natural to fear the unknown and buck the change happening all around us! But that fear can become the mountain that keeps us from moving on to the next phase of life. All too often we take our eyes off God and instead zone in on everything in front of us, allowing our fears and feelings to cripple us emotionally and physically.

The third mistake we can make is stifling our progress due to a lack of focus. In Philippians 3, Paul encourages us to keep pushing forward, as if we're running a race and heading toward the finish line. Which, of course, we all are. However, while we're on this earth and until we meet Jesus on our final day, we're still called to keep running a good race.

Life is going to move forward with or without us. We can accept change and trust God has a plan and will hold us tight and show us the way, or we can stay stuck in the past—unhappy, dissatisfied, discontent, hopeless—and paralyzed in the present. When we remain fixated on what once was, rather than thinking about what could be, not only will we miss the season we're in but we'll also be blinded to the future God has in store for us.

Transitioning well will always require a shift in perspective and focus. This allows us to move from where we are mentally to where we want to be. If we redirect our attention to Jesus rather than our circumstances and put our hope in Him, we will be filled with the peace that surpasses understanding. When our focus is right and our fear is in check, everything else will fall into place. Proverbs 3:5–6 is beautiful evidence of this promise: "Trust in the LORD with all your heart; do not depend on your own understanding. Seek his will in all you do, and he will show you which path to take."

We all can shift our thinking, which equips us to move forward, knowing He will make our paths known and trusting Him to do His work.

As an example of how these stumbling blocks can keep us from moving forward, let's think back to the story of the Israelites in Exodus, where they were constantly looking to the past. Even though their past included slavery, it had become their comfort zone. God had set them free and was leading them to the Promised Land, but because the transition was nothing like they had ever experienced before, they lost their focus on who was leading them and therefore lost their faith and trust in Him. Because they were facing so many unknowns, they were afraid and didn't have confidence in God's plans.

I recall a time when I did that, and not only during the holidays. After my marriage ended, I mourned for the days of the past even though many of those days had been spent in tears, turmoil, hurt, confusion, and fear of what was happening and what the future might bring if the worst actually did happen. The uncomfortable season I had been living in had become my comfort zone, a place of security simply because it was the only life I knew. And when God pulled me out of it, I doubted His every move.

This hurts, Lord! I didn't want this to happen to my marriage. Even though it was difficult living in a crumbling marriage, at least I had financial security. At least I knew where the next meal was coming from for my children and myself. At least it felt and looked like we were a normal family rather than a broken one.

I could go on and on with the ridiculous excuses, lies, and false beliefs I was feeding my thoughts with—all because I was terrified of the transitional period I found myself in. I was so caught up in the past and the losses I had incurred that I couldn't even fathom that the future could possibly be good, much less better.

I glamorized the past even though it wasn't worthy of it. And I certainly wasn't resting in God's promises and trusting Him with my future. I was so busy obsessing over what once was and what I had lost and being afraid of what the future held, I found myself incapable of looking ahead and seeing the future as a new beginning that was going to be blessed by a good God.

I was stuck at a crossroads between the past and the future, and I didn't know where to turn. All because I didn't know how to accept where God had me and instead allowed my fears to stand in the way and prevent me from transitioning into the next phase of my life with joy and expectation. Thankfully, in time, God opened my eyes to see life differently and trust Him fully. It didn't happen overnight, but what matters is that it did happen!

And He has blessed me immensely through each of my seasons of new beginnings.

If we redirect our attention to Jesus rather than our circumstances and put our hope in Him, we will be filled with the peace that surpasses understanding.

Let's revisit the transition the Israelites were going through as they tried to make their way to the Promised Land. They learned many lessons on that journey, all of which we can learn from today as well, the first of those being that the shortest route to what God has in store for us is not always the best route.

I've read that Moses could have made it to Canaan in about a week, but since we know it took forty years to get there, that is obviously not the route God led him down. Why? Because God had a plan—for the whole forty years. He wanted to protect His people and help them be prepared. Plus, many miracles occurred that no one could have ever imagined.

Also, had God led them on the quickest route, they would have had to pass through enemy territory. Exodus 13:17–18 reads, "When Pharaoh finally let the people go, God did not lead them along the main road that runs through Philistine territory, even though that was the shortest route to the Promised Land. God said, 'If the people are faced with a battle, they might change their minds and return to Egypt.' So God led them in a roundabout way through the wilderness toward the Red Sea." Having lived in slavery for decades, the Israelites weren't in any condition to fight a war, much less come out alive. God also knew that if they tried to move too quickly and had to face war, they would get frustrated or discouraged and not only stop in their tracks but also turn around and long for the past, even though it involved suffering and slavery. His delay and rerouting was His way of protecting them, even though they didn't realize it at the time.

In many seasons and situations, I've wondered why God waited so long to answer my prayers and why my journey was so painfully long. At times, I doubted the way He answered my prayers, which was different from what I had asked for. Maybe you have as well.

For example, when I started dreaming about being a writer, I prayed about my calling for five years, continually pitching book proposals to multiple publishers and agents at writers' conferences, only to face rejection after rejection year after year. I even put those dreams in a drawer (literally), assuming I had heard God wrong, because nothing seemed to be happening regardless of my efforts. It was like He took me on a roundabout way through my own wilderness as I waited to get a glimpse of His plans.

Then when the timing was perfect, God miraculously opened the door for my very first book contract. Had I tried to write that book five years prior, I wouldn't have had the experience, wisdom, and knowledge I had gained in the meantime. I wouldn't have been as strong in my faith, because back then I had yet to experience having to fully trust and rely on God for everything.

It certainly wasn't the shortest or most comfortable route to getting published, but it was the best route because I not only grew and matured as a woman, a believer, and a writer but also had a bank of experiences and stories that equipped me to write on my topic, which at the time was overwhelming stress, resulting in my first published book, *Stressed-Less Living*.

As another example, after my divorce, I tried to sell my house and downsize because I needed a more reasonable mortgage payment. But every time I started the process—at one point even getting as far as listing it and having a solid offer—I would find out about yet another obstacle beyond my control that prevented me from selling it. It took nearly seven years to be able to list the house free and clear, but when I finally could, the timing was perfection that I couldn't have orchestrated if I'd tried. The housing market was booming, and the value of my house had gone up drastically.

God knew that although I was frustrated with the hundreds of stumbling blocks I'd tripped over during the journey and all the seemingly never-ending legal battles I'd had to fight, the sale of that home would help provide for my financial future, which wouldn't have happened had I sold it years earlier, in my timing. In addition, I was more confident as an independent woman who could take care of hard things and more spiritually strong as a result of such a long, difficult journey. All of that helped me feel excited about moving into my new home and jump-starting a new season of life (except for that dramatic meltdown I had on moving day, of course!).

Sometimes God brings us the long way around because we aren't emotionally, mentally, or spiritually prepared to face what lies ahead. But alongside the wait will come many, many blessings, including maturity and growth.

The Israelites' roundabout journey eventually landed them at the edge of the Red Sea, and we all know what happened there. A miracle of epic proportions. God parted the sea just long enough for all of them to safely cross, then sealed the deal as He destroyed Pharaoh and his army by swallowing them up in the waters. This also closed the path to the Israelites ever being able to turn back to their uncomfortable existence, which they were remembering as a safe place and not a place of slavery. They had to keep moving and learn to trust God to provide for their every need, and as a result, they witnessed miracles and saw God's hand at work time and time again. Manna raining from the sky, quail in abundance, and Moses bringing water from a rock, to name a few.

God knew He had great plans for them, and He wanted them to experience those plans in His timing and for their own good.

Transitions can make us feel like we're wandering in the wilderness too, wondering what in the world God is up to and asking Him why we must suffer. We feel desperate for change yet powerless to make it happen. We want to know how to prosper and thrive quicker and with ease but find ourselves getting tripped up or stuck time after time. And it may seem like we're going in the wrong direction simply because we don't know how to cross over from one phase of life to the next.

Rest assured, God knows what needs to happen better than we do. He knows what the future holds and what is best for His children—including you and me. There can be many reasons our journey takes longer than we want it to or involves twists and turns we never expected. But that is for God to know and us to find out. As I mentioned in an earlier chapter, God often takes us on a journey we didn't know we needed so He can bring us everything we didn't even know we wanted. It's always up to us to trust the plan—God's plan.

Because the Israelites' transition was a long one, not only did they have to trust God with their future, but they also had to trust Him moment by moment as well. And we need to do the same, remembering that the God who performed all those miracles for the Israelites is the same God who leads us today through every circumstance.

Maybe you feel like you've been on such a long journey, much like the Israelites, and you're tired in every way. You're frustrated that God doesn't seem to be answering your prayers. You feel overlooked, forgotten, and unimportant to the One who is supposed to hold you so dear. You made plans that didn't pan out; you saw doors shut that you wanted to be open. You don't understand what God is up to, and you're wondering if you can still lean on Him and trust Him.

Sweet friend, I get it. But in times of confusion, frustration, or hopelessness, it's important we always keep in mind, especially when the road ahead looks scary, that God's plans are not our plans. We're reminded of this in Isaiah 55:8–9: "'My thoughts are nothing like your thoughts,' says the LORD. 'And my ways are far beyond anything you could imagine. For just as the heavens are higher than the earth, so my ways are higher than your ways and my thoughts higher than your thoughts.'"

Even if we don't understand (or particularly like) His plans, as we begin to advance in our journey, we can believe we're changing and growing and experiencing God in ways we wouldn't have otherwise. Having been through some tough transitions (and I've shared only a few with you), I can honestly say I wouldn't trade where God led me for anything. I wouldn't go back to my past, and I'm so happy with my life and with who I became in the process. At the time, it was scary, but now I see it was an amazing adventure.

Is life perfect now? No, but my faith is stronger, and I'm more confident in who I am and what I'm capable of. The truth is, many times hard things put us on a path toward the best things that will ever happen to us. And sometimes we need to appreciate where we are and how far we've come and simply be proud of ourselves, while recognizing we're still learning and growing.

Can you and I make a pact right now to not give up on God's plans for our new beginnings, even if we don't understand them or they seem slow in coming? If your answer is yes, close your eyes and whisper that commitment to your heavenly Father, knowing He is right by your side. He is listening and ready for you to embark on your new beginning. Then whisper it to yourself, and don't forget it.

Moving Forward

Think about It

Which of the four transitions do you feel you are in right now? What are the feelings this transition is evoking in your heart? Have you ever taken notice of your emotions and the things that trigger them and chosen to not let them rule your life? If not, contemplate what changes you could make today to stop letting your emotions derail you from your new adventure.

Plan for It

What are the stumbling blocks—whether physical, mental, or emotional—that could stand in the way of you moving forward into your new season of life? Make a list of all the things that come to mind.

Now take your list of stumbling blocks, and determine if each of your obstacles is perceived or real. If it's perceived, ask God to help you change your perspective so you can overcome that pattern of negative thinking and trust Him fully. If it's a real obstacle, craft a solid plan for how you're going to handle it should it come up in the future.

Act on It

Surrender your transition to God. The word *surrender* "implies a giving up after a struggle to retain or resist."[3] At times, we may find ourselves resisting the change and struggling to get things back to how they used to be. But it's time to trust God completely no matter the outcome because you know He is a God who provides and looks out for His children. If you made that commitment to God I suggested at the end of this chapter, consider writing it down so you don't forget it. Surrender whatever it is that you are resisting. Arise each morning, and remind yourself you won't give up on your new beginning and you will trust the One who is taking you on this journey.

If you're ready to embark on the new adventure God has in store for your life, jot down some ideas of things you can do this week to begin acting on your biggest dreams and pushing past even your biggest stumbling blocks.

Pray over It

Jesus, You know the fears in my heart and the obstacles that stand in the way of me pressing forward in this new season. You know my doubts, and I pray for the strength to push past them and not allow false beliefs or fear to hold me back from experiencing what You have in store for me. Give me the wisdom, strength, and stamina to keep running the race and pursuing the dreams I know You've put in my heart. I commit to trust You as I continue and will look for Your guidance every day. Amen.

Write your own prayer to Jesus in this space.

Chapter 6

The Key to Transitioning Well

There are three specific seasons when my self-esteem hit an all-time low, and the dismal opinions I had of myself affected me and every area of my life. Unfortunately, my lack of confidence, tangled with an abundance of shame and regret, kept me stuck with a lack of courage all the way into adulthood.

The first low season happened when I made a tragic choice as a freshman in college. Due to overwhelming fear, confusion, uncertainty, and immaturity, I opted to have an abortion to end an unplanned pregnancy. I felt so ashamed and appalled at my uneducated decision that I spent seventeen years feeling worthless, irreparably scarred, unworthy of God's love, and incapable of being redeemed, much less having any purpose in life. But God ...

Second, after I had spent seven years climbing the corporate ladder at a Big Four accounting firm, a new supervisor came onto the scene who had a demeaning, belittling, and critical management style. Nothing I did was ever good enough, and every day, I was hit with crushing criticism and unfair judgment. When I finally made the hard choice to resign because the environment was so toxic and unhealthy, my already-fragile self-esteem had shattered and felt beyond repair. I left that job feeling as if I had no good qualities whatsoever, convinced I was a complete failure. I had allowed the treatment of one person with misguided actions to affect who I believed myself to be. But God ...

Third and most recent, as I've already shared with you, my husband of twenty-five years left me for another woman who was more than two decades younger than me. He traded me, our life, and our children for what he thought looked more like what he wanted. I felt tossed aside, humiliated, useless, ugly, hopeless, unworthy, and undeserving of love. Again, I had tried and failed. Again, I had been knocked off my feet with the belief that I was worthless. For years, I thought I would never regain my confidence and self-esteem, much less love myself or my life again. But God ...

There have been plenty of other times when random strangers, so-called friends, online haters, coworkers, church members, and community members have spoken words or treated me in ways that left a trail of damage in my heart and riddled my self-esteem with holes that couldn't be filled.

The view we have of ourselves can either make us or break us, especially when we're faced with new beginnings. Strong self-esteem is the foundation for success in every season of life. You might be wondering, *How can I develop strong self-esteem when I feel so low and lost?* That's a great question and one I'm going to address in this chapter.

We all have life-changing negative experiences that we remember all too vividly. Those seasons when the damage ran so deep that it affected who we are and how we see ourselves. Sometimes traumatic child-hood experiences or the words and actions of our parents damaged our self-esteem before we even had a chance to form an opinion of ourselves in a true light. We're all shaped by the messages given to us by others over the years, and many of us still face criticism today from family members, people at work, or friends. But God ...

I've learned through all those experiences that my self-confidence and self-worth don't have to depend on what other people think, how other people treat me, or what I've done or not done.

We always have more power over ourselves than our external critics have. Human nature is such that we can be our own worst enemy because we can also be highly critical of ourselves and leave no room for self-compassion. However, we can choose to be our own biggest cheerleader instead. My ability to accomplish my dreams doesn't hinge on whether other people believe I can or not. And neither does yours. Yet we must believe that truth in order to make it a reality.

Ultimately the words we speak to ourselves carry greater weight than those from others and can have the most influence on our ability to be happy, successful, and confident.

Take a Look Inward

Maybe you have healthy self-esteem. If so, I'm happy you do! But sadly, so many beautiful, amazing, and talented people suffer from low self-esteem.[1] So for those who are struggling, let's take a moment to think about the signs of low self-esteem, which we may not have even recognized in ourselves before, and acknowledge—maybe for the first time—that it's something we have the power to change.

Signs of low self-esteem include being overly critical of yourself and saying negative things about yourself to others, even if you say them in a joking manner. If you focus on your flaws instead of all your positive traits or you ignore achievements and successes because you can't seem to believe you deserve accolades, those are red flags of low self-esteem. When you blame yourself for what someone else has done or when you think everyone is better than you and you can never measure up, low self-esteem is most likely the culprit.

Although it's basically an epidemic in today's culture, low self-esteem doesn't come without consequences. It can create anxiety, loneliness, stress, and an increased likelihood of depression. It can cause relational problems with other people, including friends, spouses, and family members. It can even impair academic or job performance. And unfortunately, if low self-esteem deepens and goes unchecked for too long, it can lead to vulnerability to substance abuse.[2]

But despite what caused our low self-esteem and how long we've lived with it, it's never too late to turn things around! Everyone wants to feel good about themselves, and everyone can.

A crucial step in truly beginning again is recognizing the lies we've believed about ourselves. A friend shared with me that she used to believe she was stupid because she was ridiculed by fellow students while learning to read in elementary school. She carried that with her until she took college classes in her forties and got straight As! It finally dawned on her that she was a smart person who believed she was stupid and had to pretend she was smart so nobody would know she was stupid. She said, "I don't think my self-esteem would have risen had I not first recognized what I thought of myself—and realized it wasn't true." Crazy! Right? But aren't we all guilty of that in one way or another?

Maybe someone didn't call you stupid but instead said you weren't pretty or didn't dress well. Perhaps they taunted you by saying you didn't have enough talent to be on a sports team you were passionate about, or maybe a parent told you you'd never amount to anything. Possibly a coworker or boss convinced you that you would never get promoted. Maybe a spouse made you feel less than wanted, and you live with the false belief that nobody could want you or see you as valuable.

False beliefs about ourselves are the enemy of new beginnings. If you're still holding on to any of those messages, it's time to stop allowing them to have an impact on your self-confidence and your life. It's time to adopt a fresh, new outlook on who you are and your worth in this world!

The second crucial step in truly beginning again is understanding your value in God's eyes. Ephesians 1:4 says, "Even before he made the world, God loved us and chose us in Christ to be holy and without fault in his eyes." People may overlook you. Pierce your heart with hurtful words or actions. Reject you. But that's okay, because the One who matters most has chosen and accepted you, on purpose, from the very start.

If you recognize your struggle with false beliefs, today can be the first day of your new and transformed mind! Whenever those beliefs start bubbling up in your heart, causing you to retreat and feel incapable of accomplishing your dreams, give yourself a little pep talk, like I used to do.

Say to yourself, "My feelings are valid, but I'm not going to sink into self-pity or continue believing something is wrong with me. I refuse to let thoughts that are not from God have any bearing. I know the One who matters the most, and He handpicked me. I may not have been chosen by others, but I am chosen by Him. I've got this because God's got me."

Over time, if you make this pep talk a habit, your attitude will begin to change. When you look in the mirror, you'll start seeing the reflection of someone you admire, believe in, and even like. Someone who is valued and loved by God and someone He has good plans for, no matter what you're going through. When your attitude changes, your life will follow suit.

The foundation of transitioning well is knowing who you are and whose you are and being proud of that person.

You don't have to be perfect to matter and have value.

We need to be acutely aware of three critical elements of self-esteem: self-respect, self-compassion, and self-awareness.

Self-respect is the regard you have for yourself. Knowing your worth and your value to others. Recognizing you are a good friend, a good mom, a good wife, a good employee, a good person in your community as a giver of your time and heart. Seeing your good traits instead of only the ones you don't like. You respect yourself when you believe you are worthy of love, happiness, friendship, and the respect of others. You must take pride in accomplishments and not let your failures derail you.

Self-compassion is simply being kind to yourself. Treat yourself just as you would treat others, with empathy, understanding, and grace.

You don't have to be perfect to matter and have value. Talk to yourself in ways you would want someone else to encourage you. Don't tear yourself down over every mistake, regret, or failure, but forgive yourself, and focus on the beautiful person God created you to be. Treat yourself like you are someone you love. Be your own best friend, first and foremost.

The third element is self-awareness, which simply means understanding yourself. How do you feel, think, behave? What are your needs, abilities, triggers? How are you letting the words or criticism of others affect who you are today? You have to understand yourself before you can see areas that are holding you back or need improvement.

Take Control of Your Self-Esteem

We can never control what other people say about us or do to us, but we can always control our interpretation of it and how we let their words affect us. And you know what? All too often, when other people judge us, say critical words, or treat us in ways that damage our self-image, they are acting out of their own low self-esteem or even jealousy. That's why it's so important to take people's words with a grain of salt instead of letting them crush us. Before we allow criticism to affect us, we can spend time pondering whether it has merit and determining if it's even worthy of our attention.

We can also control our inner critic. I mentioned earlier that we are often our own worst enemy, and it's so true. We cleave to false beliefs and allow them to grow in our minds. This tendency is basically nothing more than irrational thinking, because we aren't assessing ourselves realistically or logically. We inadvertently allow all those negative thoughts to become a habit and give us a distorted view of ourselves, which leads to low self-esteem. When we put ourselves down constantly, nobody else needs to!

Our inner critic wages psychological warfare in our heads, and that war is hard to win. It keeps us from being able to tap into the courage and confidence we need. Unless we recognize our negative thoughts and learn to challenge them, we will continue to believe them and stay stuck with low self-esteem. I don't want to live that way, and I'm sure you don't either.

So let's look at a few ways to begin shifting our self-esteem and the habitual negative thoughts that may be preventing us from accepting the new season God has in store.

Use the Thought-Capturing Approach

Second Corinthians 10:5 says, "We demolish arguments and every pretension that sets itself up against the knowledge of God, and we take captive every thought to make it obedient to Christ" (NIV). Not only is this a technique we can use, but it's also a holy command that is life changing when applied.

We can control our own thoughts, and it begins with asking Christ to help us be acutely aware of the words we say to ourselves. Each time you notice yourself thinking something negative about yourself, stop and say out loud, "I will not think that way anymore! And I am going to be compassionate and kind to little ol' me." Shift your thoughts in a different direction, and focus on something positive instead.

Think with Logic

Once you've captured a negative thought, think logically about what you just told yourself.

Where is the proof that statement is true? What is the evidence that would fully support what you're saying? Does that mistake or failure really warrant those harsh thoughts about yourself? Are you expecting perfection of yourself, which you wouldn't expect from others?

Eliminate Negative Words from Your Vocabulary

Words like *always*, *never*, and *everyone* tend to fuel that inner critic, so replace them with more realistic ones. For example, "In some situations,

I ..." or "Sometimes I ..." Rarely, if ever, are the negative things we tell ourselves true descriptions of who we are, but instead, they are reflective of a situation or circumstance.

When you find yourself using these words, especially if it's a habit, begin being conscious of replacing them with ones that offer grace and compassion to yourself. We can remind ourselves, *I may not be perfect, but parts of me are excellent.* Or, *I may have fallen short in this situation, but I rose above the rest in another.* This practice helps us acknowledge areas where we need improvement but still focus on and celebrate our strengths. Although it's often hard to give ourselves kudos for positive attributes, it's critical that we do. And when we do, especially in front of others, people learn to respect and value us even more.

Stop Comparing Yourself with Others

It's human nature to compare ourselves to others, but the result can set us up for feeling inadequate and less than. There will always be people who appear to be better, more talented, more successful, more refined, and so on, but there will also always be people who look up to you even if you don't realize it. There are people who look at you and feel less than or not as good in one way or another, and although we never want to make people feel that way or treat anyone in that manner, we can use it as a reminder that we may not be at the top of our game but we're also not at the bottom and there are people who look up to us, just as we look up to others.

Remember who God made you to be. Love who you see in the mirror. Be true to yourself. Always live up to your own expectations, not the perceived expectations of others, and stop letting comparison eat away at your self-esteem and confidence, which keeps you from being all you can be.

Surround Yourself with Positive People

As much as possible, it's important to disengage with people who habitually make you feel inferior, put you down, and/or are highly critical and negative. Do yourself a favor, and begin setting boundaries and choosing wisely who you agree to spend time with, which should be people who bring joy to your heart, not discouragement or feelings of inferiority. Begin to take notice of people who seem to have a healthy self-esteem and who treat others with admiration and respect; then try to surround yourself with that type of person. As my friend Lysa TerKeurst once said, "All relationships can be *difficult* at times, but they should not be *destructive* to our well-being."[3] And for that matter, they should not be destructive to our self-esteem either. Our self-esteem is related to our well-being because it helps us feel more self-confident.

You may not be able to remove all negative people from your life, especially if they are in your workplace or inside your own home. But knowing who you are and believing in your value, as well as incorporating some of the practices I've shared in this chapter, can give you the inner strength to avoid letting their critical words or harsh treatment impact your self-esteem. And remember, their words reflect who they are, not who you are.

Love Yourself

This tip is easier said than done. Yet it's a holy command, as Jesus explains in Matthew 22:37–40: "'You must love the LORD your God with all your heart, all your soul, and all your mind.' This is the first and greatest commandment. A second is equally important: 'Love your neighbor as yourself.' The entire law and all the demands of the prophets are based on these two commandments."

We've all likely read this passage before, but often we forget the significance it holds for our lives. We can't love others as Jesus wants us to until we love ourselves as Jesus loves us. Yet despite its importance, we are all likely guilty of having an adversarial relationship with ourselves, and that is not how Jesus wants us to think.

We can acknowledge all the parts of ourselves—our feelings, thoughts, actions, appearance, successes, failures—but we don't have to allow them to define who we are. They are only part of us, and the most important part of us is our identity in Christ. Matthew 10:31 reminds us, "Don't be afraid; you are more valuable to God than a whole flock of sparrows."

Because we matter to God, He can repair our brokenness.

Because we matter to God, He can turn our pain into purpose.

Because we matter to God, He can remove our shame and fill us with wholeness and self-worth.

Because we matter to God, He can redeem our circumstances and help us learn to believe in ourselves and see the value He sees in us.

And because we matter to God, He can replace our fear with courage and confidence. And courage is what we all need to transition well and pursue our visions and dreams of who we want to be and how we want our lives to be.

Be a Giver

We all know it feels good to give. When we do something kind for someone, it feels nice and our hearts swell. Studies have shown that helping other people causes a rush of endorphins in our brains, which brings on positive physiological changes. And while performing any act of selfless giving or helping, we tend to forget our own problems and increase our gratitude, which fosters self-esteem.[4]

The Bible also states the importance of giving in many places, including Isaiah 58:10: "Feed the hungry, and help those in trouble. Then your light will shine out from the darkness, and the darkness around you will be as bright as noon." When we have love and compassion for others, give selflessly, pour into other people's lives, and help others in times of need, even in the smallest of ways, the light of God within us becomes brighter and brighter, and that light can gradually help us learn to love ourselves more—if for no other reason than that God's love for us is immeasurable.

Beginning again and being in a period of uncertainty can feel scary and intimidating. It can feel disappointing and frustrating. It can seem like the end of something, instead of the start of something fresh and new. All of which can affect how we feel about ourselves and keep us from transitioning well.

Yet, in most instances, getting pushed out of our comfort zone is a good thing, even if we can't see it at the time. Not only does it force us to move forward, but it also allows us to think about who we are and who we want to be. It's another opportunity to begin looking at that woman in the mirror with a brand-new perspective—one filled with love, self-respect, self-compassion, and self-awareness. And in doing so, we are allowing ourselves to dream about, instead of dread, all the changes and blessings God has in store for us.

Moving Forward

Think about It

What are the major events in your life that left you reeling with low self-esteem or feelings of worthlessness? What are the false beliefs you've been carrying around for years that have had a greater impact on your self-esteem than you may have ever realized until now? How have these false beliefs about yourself kept you from being who you want to be, pressing through this hard season, and/or achieving the things you'd like achieve? How might they be standing in the way of you embracing your season of new beginnings and believing you've got what it takes to succeed and be happy?

I know that's a lot of questions to ponder, but you will benefit greatly from taking time to think about and answer each one. If we want to move forward with confidence, we need to identify the false beliefs holding us back from who we long to become and make a solid commitment to no longer let them keep us captive.

Plan for It

Transfer each of the questions above to your journal, or write them below, and write down your reflective answers to each one. Let your answers sink into your mind. If you've grown to believe any lies about yourself, recognize that these thoughts have power over your life. Then make a list of five to ten positive traits about yourself. Make another list of five to ten things you've accomplished that you are proud of. And if you can think of more than ten, then keep building your lists! I bet you rock more than you even realized!

Act on It

When someone crushes you with critical words or harsh treatment or makes you feel inferior or unsure about yourself or when those false beliefs you've identified try to creep into your mind, pull out your list of positive traits from above. Read them, reread them, memorize them, and tuck them into your heart. Just because you have a bad day doesn't mean every day is bad. Those days when someone hurts your feelings or you start doubting yourself or God can be turned around when you choose to focus on who you are and the words God would use to describe you according to His Word.

Consider taking your lists of positive traits and accomplishments and putting them somewhere you can see them every day to remind yourself you are worthy, loved, and wonderful in many ways! Hang them on your refrigerator, your bathroom mirror, or the wall in your office. Let these lists be your daily boost of self-confidence. The more you begin to believe in your worth, the more you can accomplish, and the more you will enjoy life overall.

Pray over It

Lord, help me remember that I am a valuable treasure in Your eyes. Feed me through Your Word all the truths You say about me, and help me let go of any messages from my past or false beliefs that are preventing me from embracing this new season of life. Help me transform my thought patterns so I can shift my perspective about myself and my capabilities as well as thrive during all transitions. Amen.

Write your own prayer to Jesus in this space.

Chapter 7

With Courage Comes Confidence

> You know, sometimes all you need is twenty seconds
> of insane courage. Just literally twenty seconds of just
> embarrassing bravery. And I promise you, something
> great will come of it.[1]

That quote is from a 2011 movie titled *We Bought a Zoo*, which is a
story about a man named Benjamin whose wife had passed away. He had
no idea how to move on with his life or how to adapt to a new lifestyle
as a widower and single dad of two. Their family was in turmoil, and
Benjamin realized there were too many memories around, haunting them
each day, and they desperately needed a change.

After looking at various homes and becoming frustrated with his
search, he finally found a large old house. His realtor tried to dissuade
him from considering it, but Benjamin decided it was perfect for his family and they would work on fixing it up. Then he found out the catch and
why the realtor was hesitant. To get the house, he also had to buy the zoo

on the property, which had closed several years earlier. He thought about it for a moment, then said to his realtor, "Why not?"

If mourning the loss of their mom wasn't enough, the children were having a hard time adjusting to a new area, new schools, and new friends. All of which eventually erupted into some family issues, as you can imagine, which prompted Benjamin to share with his son this thought about courage and the importance of even just twenty seconds of it.

In the movie, Benjamin also shared that he realized that instead of trying to forget his wife, he simply needed to accept that she would always be a part of him but that it was okay to embrace the season of transition he was in.

That is a lesson we can all take to heart, my friend. Maybe you didn't want to leave the season of life you were in, or maybe you did, but that—your past—will always be a part of who you are. But in order to make the most of the life ahead, which can happen only when you trust God enough to muster up at least twenty seconds of insane courage day after day, you have to be willing to have an open heart and mind about the new adventures God has waiting, even if they seem risky.

However, let me be the first to share that if there is one thing people have never called me, it's a risk-taker. I despise roller coasters, you won't find me at the end of a hiking trail fearlessly taking in the view from the edge of a cliff, and you certainly won't see me jumping out of a perfectly good airplane just for fun. I never really considered myself someone with courage.

But as I recently began to ponder courage, I saw something in myself I had never noticed before. Over many years, during times when I faced the choice of either dealing with my problems and circumstances or letting them bury me and I had to push past my worst fears, insecurities, and weaknesses, maybe, just maybe, I've always had a little bit of courage in me after all—doses of God's strength I didn't even realize He was giving me.

For starters, years ago as a thirty-something new mom, I attended a Christian women's conference for the very first time. The speaker spoke transparently and vulnerably, her message cracking open my heart and compelling me to face my own inner demons. Although it wasn't fun, it opened the door for God's forgiveness, healing, and redemption to finally sink into my heart once and for all.

The last conference session ended with an invitation to come forward and pray at the foot of two large wooden crosses. We were asked to write our worst shame or sin on a note card, whatever it was that made us feel worthless and unlovable in the eyes of God. Then we were to pick up a hammer and nail that note card to the cross. It was a public act of totally surrendering my sin and shame so Jesus could carry them instead of me.

As I sat at my table, like a deer in the headlights after hearing the instructions, I couldn't move. I felt paralyzed in my seat, as if my legs were jelly. What if someone saw what I wrote on my note card? What if people wondered why I was a blubbering mess? What if I was judged? What if someone watched and whispered in another's ear?

I had zero ounces of courage to get up and move. Until I did.

From somewhere deep inside my soul, a holy courage began bubbling up to the surface. The Holy Spirit was relentlessly nudging me to follow what my heart was telling me to do. To the point where I couldn't have stayed seated if I had wanted to. I stood, with wobbly knees and tears streaming down my face, walked from the back of a huge hotel ballroom to the stage, waited my turn in a long line of tearful attendees, then knelt, prayed, and physically nailed my sin to the cross. This small act of courage shifted the course of my entire life.

Months later, I began volunteering at a crisis pregnancy center, encouraging young women to choose life for their unborn children. Each time I was scheduled to meet with a new client, I was terrified. Who was I to minister to these young women? All those false beliefs I had surrendered to Christ on that wooden cross came crashing back in, the Enemy trying to convince me I couldn't do what I felt called to do because of sins in my own past. So each time before I met with another scared, broken young woman, I prayed fervently for courage and the right words to share and that God would keep her from seeing my tears as my heart broke for hers.

I still smile at the thought that there are amazing women and men walking around today who may not have been given a chance to live if not for my tiny acts of courage during that time. I obeyed God's call to volunteer, even though it was scary and I felt completely unqualified and unequipped.

Another example is that, after that experience, God impressed another calling on my heart. I felt called to become a speaker, to share my story and help other women discover the power of God's healing and how He can turn their past into their purpose, just as He had done for me.

There was a reason I was sitting in the back of the ballroom during that conference, keeping to myself. I liked being a wallflower. I had always been the shy, introverted type and could barely even speak up in meetings at work. Despite knowing that God was calling me to go and share, the whole "stand on the stage with all eyes on me" speaker gig felt like a crippling, ridiculous idea. I was terrified at the thought of sharing my story and being transparent with all the women sitting in the audience.

Yet somehow God gave me the courage to do exactly that. At the first speaking event I was ever invited to, I sat in the car for an hour in the rain, too afraid to go in. But when I finally did, God's courage took over. I took a deep breath and walked onto the stage, despite being filled with a desire to run and hide behind the piano. But as soon as I started sharing, God's strength within me started soaring. Afterward, I put in the effort to create a new beginning for myself, and over time, my speaking ministry grew, as well as my courage and confidence.

I then felt called to write my first book because even though I didn't consider myself a writer, I knew that God had laid it on my heart to use the power of written words to share what He had done in my life. I prayed for Him to give me the words He wanted me to write, and He did exactly that. I did it only out of obedience and through the courage and power of the Holy Spirit within me. Each of the seven books I've written since then has stemmed from a hard transition period. I can see the fingerprints of God, and I can also see how He has used my obedience in the lives of many, which has made every hard transition and every difficult experience worth it.

It took courage to quit my full-time job because of the treatment I was receiving from my boss. I had to accept the reality of losing my entire salary and my identity as an executive, but I knew that God was calling me into ministry, even though at the time I had absolutely no idea what it would look like. God provided for my family in miraculous ways and also opened doors that never would have opened had I not embraced this new phase and trusted He would lead the way.

It took courage to end a broken marriage after twenty-five years and stop being an enabler of unacceptable behavior. It was the worst and most terrifying of new beginnings, but I knew the time had come to put myself, my children, my future, and my happiness as my first priorities. It was a mortifying risk I never wanted to take, and it wasn't easy, but I made it through, and as I've already shared, I am happier and more secure now than ever before.

It took courage to begin doing simple new things like learning to play golf and continuing to play while trying to improve, despite discovering that it isn't really a talent I possess. There is definitely no chance of me joining the LPGA anytime soon!

It took courage to step out in faith and begin my own coaching business for aspiring writers (traciemiles.com) with no assurance it would succeed. But God had given me a passion to help other writers follow His call on their lives and use their stories for His glory, so I moved forward in blind faith and now have a thriving business of helping impassioned and enthusiastic writers who dream of getting published.

It took courage to begin delving into real estate investing when I had no experience or knowledge in that field at all, not to mention no real funds to support such a venture. I spent a year reading books, listening to podcasts, and soaking in everything I could learn from online community groups. In time, God paved the way, provided what I needed, and opened doors for me to get started, with one house flip, a short-term rental property, and another house flip currently underway. I had a dream of what I wanted to do and committed to doing whatever it took to keep pushing forward, trying to build a secure financial future for myself and my family.

I began to travel more and take chances on getting out of the comfort zone of my small community, even going on an impromptu trip to London,

England, for a few days with my daughter and best friend. Which turned out to be one of the best spontaneous decisions I'd ever made! Being the type of person who likes to have plans, spreadsheets, and itineraries for everything I do, I learned that overthinking and overanalyzing everything can rob us of so many amazing experiences. Sometimes we just have to say yes and take a chance on ourselves!

You see, He gave me the courage to do things I didn't even know I had in me. In every circumstance, He gave me hope and dreams for the future, and I wanted them to become a reality. I took risks I never thought I would take, and it all started because I simply decided to begin again with each endeavor.

Let's go back to my original statement. I really am not a risk-taker. I've never been an overly confident person, much less a courageous person. But with each little step I took in the strength of the Holy Spirit alone, in the smallest of situations and the most difficult circumstances, I tapped into holy courage, which helped me build confidence, not only in God but also slowly in myself.

One of the greatest ways to build confidence is to act like we already have it and simply go with it. Or is that called courage? Hmm.

Confidence and Courage Aren't the Same

Many people think confidence and courage are the same thing or that self-confidence must come first, which then fuels our courage. But indeed, it's exactly the opposite.

Confidence is a belief in our own abilities, qualities, or traits. It's the feeling of self-assurance and trust in ourselves that makes us hold our heads high and live without fear of judgment or failure, because we believe in who we are. Confidence is often the result of experience, wisdom, and knowledge we've gained and success in past undertakings.

Courage, on the other hand, is the ability to face fear, danger, or uncertainty with bravery and determination. It's the willingness to take chances and to act despite fear or adversity and despite how many unknowns lie ahead. Courage involves overcoming obstacles each time they roll into our paths, and it requires a certain level of strength and resilience. Courage opens the door for you to be an active participant in living your life to the fullest as it is, while working hard to improve it.

To sum it up, confidence is believing in ourselves and what we are capable of in Christ, and courage is the ability to act on what we want to do because we believe in ourselves. We can build confidence through experience and success, while courage often requires wandering outside of our comfort zones and being willing to take the risks we feel God is calling us to take.

None of the examples I mentioned earlier from my own journey could have happened of my own accord. It was an all-powerful God who instilled courage in me that propelled me to do daunting things. And with each small act of courage, my confidence grew, a new beginning blossomed, and I got the blessing of seeing God at work in my life.

Scripture provides many examples of courageous men and women who achieved amazing things—not because they didn't feel scared, frustrated, ill equipped, or unworthy but because they believed God was who He said He was and they put their future in His hands.

Esther serves as a great example of someone moving forward fearlessly in courage and confidence because of her faith alone.

She was a young Jewish woman living in Persia who found favor with the king, then became queen, and then risked her life to save the Jewish people from destruction after a court official manipulated the king into authorizing their demise. She was asked by her cousin Mordecai to go to the king and beg him to save her people. At that time, approaching the king without an invitation was a crime punishable by death, but from somewhere deep down inside, she mustered up the holy courage and confidence to do exactly that.

She had her cousin's support and encouragement, and he told her, "If you keep quiet at a time like this, deliverance and relief for the Jews will arise from some other place, but you and your relatives will die. Who knows if perhaps you were made queen for just such a time as this?" (Est. 4:14).

Esther had to choose to walk into the unknown, regardless of how things turned out, and her actions had an impact not only on her future but also on countless others'. Her twenty seconds of courage in talking to the king saved her people and made history.

Moses had to face his fears and insecurities when he heard God's command to rescue His people from Egypt and lead them to the Promised Land. He even questioned God's plan in Exodus 3:11–12:

> Moses protested to God, "Who am I to appear before Pharaoh? Who am I to lead the people of Israel out of Egypt?"
>
> God answered, "I will be with you. And this is your sign that I am the one who has sent you: When you have brought the people out of Egypt, you will worship God at this very mountain."

Moses had to have confidence in who God was so he could unearth the courage to do as God asked. His bravery inspired the Jews to follow him out of slavery and experience the parting of the Red Sea. One small act of courage made history.

Think about David in 1 Samuel, where the Israelites and Philistines were at war, keeping in mind David wasn't even a part of the army and certainly wasn't a trained soldier. He was present only because his father, Jesse, had asked him to deliver supplies to his older brothers and return with an update on how the battle was going.

All the big and mighty soldiers fled and cowered at the size of their enemy, Goliath, who was "six cubits and a span" (17:4 NIV), which is approximately nine feet, nine inches tall. But David had the courage to stand up and fight. Despite Saul taunting David and telling him he was too young to fight in battle, much less take on Goliath, he did it anyway.

David knew something the soldiers didn't. His confidence, strength, and courage came from God, not himself. He had confidence in his skills; however, he knew that the true source of his courage to do what seemed impossible was his faith, and that small, faith-fueled act of courage made history.

All three of these examples have important aspects in common. First, each of them had to draw on a courage beyond themselves to do the hard things God put in front of them. Second, regardless of their fears, insecurities, and objections, and even at the risk of their lives, each of them showed bravery and chose to act. They chose to move forward into whatever the future held for them because they trusted their God, and as a result, they were filled with holy confidence and courage. And third, each of them had to move out of their comfort zone.

Get Out of Your Comfort Zone

Moving out of our comfort zone—especially in a difficult season—can seem harder than anything else. But our comfort zone is a place where spirits get crushed. A place where dreams and visions die. A place where joy can become stifled. A place where hopelessness about the future and disappointment about the past and present can take root. A place that can paralyze us if we let it.

Our comfort zone is a dangerous place that can keep us from being all we can be, doing all we can do, and enjoying the blessings God has in store for us. But that doesn't have to be my fate or yours. We can have the courage to cross over into our new reality, accept change, and trust that God is leading us into new territories and adventures.

Choosing to be brave, or at least being willing to muster up twenty seconds of insane courage like I already mentioned, can make a world of difference. Once we take those brave, fearless steps, our confidence begins to grow, and life will change. We will change too, from the inside out, as we shift our perspectives about new beginnings, whether we wanted them to happen or not.

God is always with you, and He will show you the way.

Like Esther, you were made for such a time as this. God placed you in this unfamiliar season or period of transition for a reason; it's not just somewhere you randomly ended up. You are about to do incredible things with your bravery, maybe even make history.

Like Moses, you may feel unqualified to tackle the unknowns of the future. You may feel incapable of doing hard things, taking chances, and trusting God to show you the way. You may feel small, insignificant, and ill equipped. But God is always with you, and He will show you the way.

And like David, maybe you're in a spot you never thought you would be in. A place you don't think you even belong, but here you are. With a dream to do something amazing. A vision to do something beyond your wildest dreams. A desire to make a difference in the world in whatever way God has placed on your heart. You've entered a massive restructuring phase, and you're putting the pen to a blank piece of paper, ready to map out your next adventure. God has you right where you're supposed to be, and He will give you the courage and confidence to make headway—but first you must start making things happen.

Diana Ross is a great example of this. She was an American singer and actress who rose to fame as the lead singer of the Supremes, which eventually became Motown's most successful act and the bestselling female vocal group during the 1960s. Most people don't know she had some of that insane courage I've been talking about. All odds were against her, but she knew what it would take to make her dreams come true—and she did it. What did she do? She set goals and pursued them. She had a vision of what she wanted, and she never let herself lose sight of it. She didn't give up. She turned her fantasies into realities. Now almost eighty years old, Diana has accomplished more than she ever dreamed. In fact, she made history too.

Diana once said, "You can't just sit there and wait for people to give you that golden dream, you've got to get out there and make it happen for yourself."[2] So true!

This is your time to choose to start making your dreams happen. Your time to move forward, face your biggest fears, accept where God has you, allow yourself to dream, embrace the new season you're embarking on, and start making things happen. Over time, you'll see your fantasies begin morphing into realities too.

Sometimes one simple act or just twenty seconds of faith-fueled courage can catapult you into the new beginning you've been longing for. Choose the life you want, and run in that direction. Don't settle for anything less. And remember, God's got you and you're going to be okay.

Moving Forward

Think about It

Look back at your life for a few minutes, and consider what you have done that took courage. What risks have you taken that opened new doors and helped you mature and learn? How did it make you feel to accomplish something you weren't sure you had the ability to do? Did your confidence grow once you achieved success in some area?

How might the season of change you are in right now look different if you tapped into that courage, believed in yourself, trusted that God has your back, and leaped forward in blind faith?

Plan for It

What are the dreams and visions you have for your future? Take out a piece of paper, and write out exactly what you'd like your life to look like, how you hope to feel, and what you want to achieve. Kind of like a vision board. It doesn't have to be a huge dream that seems beyond you (but it could be!). It could simply be a vision you have for your future. What needs to start changing right now so you can begin beginning again?

Act on It

Start thinking about what it will take to make your vision of your
ideal future come true. Wake up each morning and give yourself
a pep talk by saying, "I've got this, and I can do this, because
God's got me!" Whatever your "this" is, it's what will motivate you
to embark on your new beginning. Hold your head high with confidence, muster up your courage, and take those first steps.

Pray over It

Lord, please fill me with confidence in myself, and help me trust You enough not only to have the courage to do the hard things and face the hard things but also to have peace along the way. Help me see myself through Your eyes and trust that You will give me whatever it takes to begin again and succeed. Help me always remember You've got me, You hear and see me, and You have a perfect plan for my future. Give me ears to hear Your whispers of guidance all along the way. Amen.

Write your own prayer to Jesus in this space.

Chapter 8

Time to Adopt a New Perspective

Marie Kondo began working as a professional tidy-upper in Japan at age nineteen, when she started tidying up her friends' homes for extra cash. She then had a dream to write a book about her passion for tidying. She believed in herself, and others believed in her and her dream as well.

An editor at Sunmark, a Japanese publishing house, worked with her for eight months, then published her now-famous book, *The Life-Changing Magic of Tidying Up: The Japanese Art of Decluttering and Organizing*, which has sold millions of copies around the world and has been translated into forty-four languages. She became a popular television show guest and starred in the 2019 Netflix show *Tidying Up with Marie Kondo*, followed in 2021 by a new Netflix show called *Sparking Joy with Marie Kondo.*[1]

Marie's philosophy of tidying wasn't to simply figure out what you don't want or need anymore and throw those things away. Rather, it was to figure out what brings you joy, then keep those things while letting the rest go.

But it's not Marie's tidying expertise, philosophy, fame, or successes that caught my attention. My interest in her was sparked when I heard that she was making a major transition because, simply put, her life had changed and she had changed as well.

In 2023, Marie announced to the public that she was no longer interested in or obsessed with tidying up. She was no longer concerned with perfectly folded laundry and towels and pristinely organized pantries. Her declaration likely resulted in an international gasp and drew lots of attention. In short, with three children in tow, she found herself living an excessively busy life and having trouble keeping up with everything, so she decided to give up on tidying and change direction. She had learned what it was like to have two kids crying on the floor because they were hungry, with another perched on her hip as she tried to cook dinner without burning it while avoiding tripping over toys and ignoring the piles of dishes in the sink.

She wanted things to be clean and still believed in her talents and the value of cleanliness, but she was in a new season, a new phase of life as a working mom, and she had a choice to make. I can only imagine that choice felt a little risky and scary considering her public image.

A *Washington Post* article stated, "The ever-organized Kondo, it seems, is a bit frazzled since giving birth to her third child in 2021." Marie herself then shared with them, "My home is messy, but the way I am spending my time is the right way for me at this time at this stage of my life."[2]

Either Marie could wallow in how she couldn't keep up with her former tidying habits and beat herself up for not being a perfect mom, housekeeper, and celebrity, or she could make changes in herself and in her life and accept this season of new circumstances with a smile on her face and joy in her heart.

She shifted her perspective about the present so she could embrace the future with open hands, something it seems she never thought she would do. She let go of who she was to reinvent who she wanted to be. She envisioned the future she wanted for herself and her family, and she turned that vision into reality.

The moral of this story is that even though we aren't Marie Kondo, maybe not famous or rich or successful to her level, we can all accept the challenge to embrace where we are, shift our perspectives, and start living differently—in ways that make us happy now and will lead to happiness in the future. We can dig deep and find the courage to pursue even the wildest of dreams if we are serious about wanting to make them happen. Once we accept that challenge, we can set attainable yet high-reaching goals and begin working toward them. We can set aside our insecurities and fears of change and create a new life for ourselves if we put our minds to it.

It all boils down to adjusting our perspectives, setting goals for ourselves, tapping into our confidence and courage, and taking action to make those goals happen.

I have no way of knowing how Marie structured her transition, but life had thrown her into a new season in which she was struggling, and she clearly knew she needed to rearrange her priorities or things would only get worse—or at best remain in a state of chaos and misery. She chose to be excited about her season of transition, to look for the positives, and to turn her fantasy of being a devoted, non-tidying mom into a reality.

Instead of staying stuck in her uncomfortable comfort zone, where she was drowning, and trying to avoid accepting that life had changed, she adjusted her outlook, set goals for what she wanted, and steamed full force ahead to achieve them. As she said in the article, things are a little bit messier now than they used to be, but she is happy with the changes she made for herself and her family.

Marie turned what may have seemed like a pipe dream—putting aside her perfectly tidy house, her lifestyle, and the art of keeping up her flawless, famous appearance—into reality through shifting her perspective, committing to perseverance, and building up the determination to create the life she really wanted, even if it meant a great deal of change. In essence, she had to begin again, and she did it well.

We can do the same in our own lives. Change is inevitable, but whether we change with it is up to us. And if life hasn't changed but you long for it to, the power is in your hands. If you're ready to begin turning your dreams and fantasies into reality, I believe in you, and you can do this! But setting goals needs to become one of your main priorities to get the ball rolling.

Without a focus on goals and ambitions, we don't have a clear thought process and we have no idea where we're going or what we want to accomplish. And sometimes we don't even know why we want what we think we want. And then, even if we do know where we're going, we don't know how to get there or what might stand in the way, which leads us to feeling stressed, overwhelmed, and disappointed and keeps us from moving forward at all!

If we aren't intentional about setting ourselves up to create the future we long for, we'll most likely end up someplace we don't want to be. This is why I wanted to focus on helping you set goals that will enable you to transition well and achieve your dreams and deepest desires. Goals aren't only for the new year; they are crucial for every aspect of life, especially when it has changed and we're embarking on a brand-new journey in a new season.

I'm going to help you start creating a blueprint for your season of transition and your future. But before setting those goals, let's look at something important: taking time to pray and figure out your *what* and your *why*.

Your *What* and Your *Why*

When facing times of change, it's easy to sit around and wish things were different. But many times, we don't really know what we're wishing for. What exactly do we want to change so we can be happier and more fulfilled? What emotional, intellectual, or physical changes do we long for? What relational desires do we have that we may not want to share with anyone? What new business venture do we dream of starting? What hobbies would we love to pick up? What financial goals do we want to hit but feel are beyond our capabilities? What will it take to begin turning some of our dreams, ambitions, and wishes into reality?

When you take time to figure out exactly what your *what* is—that thing, that change, that new beginning you want most out of life—and allow yourself to believe it can come true, you can begin thinking about a plan for how to make it happen. Keeping your *what* in mind will also influence your decisions as you begin making progress toward that goal and working toward your new beginning, new life, and new you.

Then ponder the deep roots for *why* you want that change to occur. Defining our *why* for any goal is what fuels our motivation to do anything. Whether your goal is to lose weight, start a new career, master a new skill, reach a certain financial level, overcome heartbreak and reclaim your joy, or push past a failure or disappointment, just having that as a set goal is a game changer.

Our *why* is the foundation and the vehicle that carries us along any path we want to take in our new season. Without knowing our *why*, we won't have the inner drive to do the work it takes to achieve our goals. We'll falter when we encounter inevitable obstacles. I'm sure you'll agree that everything needs a defined purpose. Otherwise, why do it at all? Knowing why we're striving so hard to accomplish something and why we want it so badly will also help us keep going when we feel like giving up.

After you've determined your *what* and your *why*, it's time to get serious about setting goals that will change your life from this day forward! I pray your heart is skipping a beat at the thought! But before we get into some serious goal setting in the next chapter, let's talk about the obvious that is probably lurking in the back of your mind. *What about all the obstacles I'll need to overcome to make my dreams, visions, and fantasies come true? How can I overcome my fears and insecurities to pursue the calling God has placed on my heart? Can the changes I'm hoping for really happen?*

Sometimes we face obstacles we can't control, and we have to figure out how to work around them so they don't hinder our progress. But many times, the biggest struggle we need to overcome is in our own minds.

We all struggle with self-defeating perspectives at times, especially when we look at our current reality and can't even fathom how things can be different, much less better. All too often we let that negativity and discouragement become a wall in our minds, especially if the situation we find ourselves in seems so far from where we want to be. Unfortunately, as a result, we waste energy on destructive and self-perpetuating thinking patterns.

I certainly am the poster child for the mental battles that stand in the way of our dreams and keep us from pursuing what God has called and equipped us to overcome and achieve. I realized this a few years ago right after my marriage had fallen apart. My thoughts were killing me and running my entire life. Yes, my circumstances were horrific, my heart was broken, every day felt like another train wreck, there were problems around every corner, and fear was overwhelming.

But one day I was so tired of feeling afraid, defeated, sad, and hopeless that I was willing to do whatever it took to create change in that season. I was exhausted and desperately wanted my heart and my circumstances to be different. I didn't want to go backward or stay stuck. I just wanted to know how to go forward.

I realized I had a decision to make: either remain pessimistic and angry about my circumstances or transform my thought patterns, trust God, and commit to being happy wherever He had me. I needed to start working on creating the future I wanted to live in, not just wishing it would happen. Intentionally doing that helped me start seeing *beginning again* with a new perspective.

Getting Out of Our Own Way

So how do we get out of our own way and change our perspectives? How do we overcome our patterns of thinking and tear down the mental walls standing in our way? How do we get unstuck and start moving forward with who we want to be and what we want to see happen in our lives?

How do we take those leaps of faith despite the uncertainties and trust that God has a plan and a beautiful future in store for us?

You know how? Decide today that you will partner with God in this journey. We may not feel capable of changing the way we think, and I realize how hard it is to break old habits. Yet God promised in His Word that transforming our thoughts is possible with Him (2 Cor. 10:5). We simply have to believe it's possible, trusting that God has us in His hands and wants the best for us. Here are a few strategies you can start implementing to help you open the door for God to steer you toward your beautiful new beginning:

1. **Surrender control.** Recognize that you can't control everything in your life and that ultimately God can. Trusting God with your future means surrendering your desires and plans to Him. However, keep in mind that surrendering control doesn't mean we sit by and just wait for the things we want to happen to happen. We still have to put in the work for God to bless it.

2. **Develop a relationship with God.** Spend time reading the Bible, praying, and attending church to deepen your relationship with God. This will equip you to understand His character better and trust His plans for you. The benefit is that, at some point, God will whisper to your spirit, and you'll know it's Him because you've come to recognize His voice, which will give you affirmation that He is indeed in control and knows the desires of your heart.

3. **Reflect on God's faithfulness.** Look back, and think about all the times when God has been faithful. Consider making a list of answered prayers. Journal about the times when you felt God wasn't at work but later, when the timing was right, He came through and you could see He had a plan all along. Think about the times when God turned something difficult or painful into something good, bringing beauty from the ashes as only He could do. Remembering how God has provided for you in the past can help you create new thought habits and give you confidence in His provision and plans for the future.

4. **Focus on the present.** Instead of worrying about what the future holds, focus on the present moment and the tasks at hand. Think about what brings you happiness right now, and make those things a priority. Remember, no matter what happens today, we must never stop believing we will make it through. And tomorrow is another new day in which we can start fresh with a positive perspective.

5. **Seek wise counsel.** Talk to trusted friends, family members, or mentors who can provide guidance and support as you navigate your future. Ask for their prayers and wisdom. Having a team of supporters, or even just one treasured friend, can help us get through the hardest and scariest of days.

6. **Practice gratitude.** Take time each day to reflect on the blessings God has bestowed on you, big and small, and thank Him for them. Thank Him for this hard season (even though it's hard!), and ask Him to help you be aware of how you can learn and grow from it. This can help you cultivate a mindset of trust and thankfulness. Take time to look around you and appreciate what you have, because some things might look very different a year down the road.

7. **Believe in yourself.** If you don't think you can do it (whatever *it* is), you certainly won't be able to. Our thoughts drive our emotions, which drive our actions. If we think negatively, we'll act negatively and reap the repercussions of our negative mindset. Our actions are what determine our destinies. Nothing will change until our mindset changes. Remember, it's not who you are that holds you back; it's who you think you're not.

8. **Talk to yourself.** Talk yourself up instead of down, and be your own best friend. When you arise every morning, notice the thoughts swirling through your mind, because everything you do all day is going to be reflective of that mindset. Tell yourself positive things. Every morning. Then repeat those confidence-boosting thoughts all day. Once you decide to do so and make that practice a habit,

throughout the day you'll make smaller decisions that line up with that optimism, which will create positive changes in your heart, mind, and life. You'll always be who you tell yourself you are. As your inner reality changes, your outer reality will follow.

9. **Choose your identity.** When you start your day, choose what kind of person you want to be, and consistently act as if you are already that person. Decide who you really want to be; then look in the mirror to see if that's who you are. Think about what changes you need to make to be the best version of yourself.

10. **Inventory your experience.** Look back, and take stock of all you've been through and all you've accomplished—despite your mistakes and failures—and be proud of who you are. Look back at what got you to where you are today; then reset your focus on where you want to be. Remember, there is a past version of you who is so proud of how far you've already come.

If you continue doing all the tips mentioned above, I promise you'll look back eventually and realize you are who you are because you showed up every single day with a positive outlook and optimism about a plan for moving forward. Great things happen as a result of taking small steps every single day.

Partnering with God on this journey and trusting Him with our future is a process, and it may take time to develop a deep and abiding faith in this area. Nobody likes not knowing what's in store or feeling pushed out of their comfort zone. Yet if we know God is leading and participating in our quest to create a better future for ourselves, we can be filled with peace and joy along the way.

Great things happen as a result of taking small steps every single day.

One of the biggest invisible hurdles we must overcome is often nothing more than the fact that we failed to put a solid plan in place. We dreamed. We wished. We fantasized. We hoped for happy new beginnings. But we didn't plan for them. We simply wanted things to happen the way we wanted them to. We wished things were different but didn't act to make those wishes come true. We don't have the blueprint we need for building the life we want or a way to track progress or celebrate accomplishments, all of which motivates us to keep persevering.

Can I encourage you to start praying for God to fill you with such passion about the dream He has given you that nothing will hold you back or obstruct your success? Just think about how you're going to feel when you reach your goals—when they are no longer a dream but a reality! Then consistently ask yourself if what you're doing each day is getting you closer to where you want to be tomorrow. If not, make the adjustments needed, and keep on trucking.

It's time to start planning for your life. Because if you don't run your life, your life will run you. *You* are the best project you will ever work on. Every single morning, you have a new opportunity to become a better version of yourself and draw closer to the life you're dreaming of.

Moving Forward

Think about It

Time for some serious self-reflection. Ponder your *what* and *why*. Doing so helps you start this journey on the right foot. To get your thoughts flowing, think about this simple example:

> What do I want? I want to lose weight. Why? Because I want my clothes to fit. Why? Because I want to look and feel good. Why? Because I want to be healthy. Why? Because I want to have energy. Why? Because I want to thrive and achieve my goals. Why? Because I want to make a difference in the world and be a good example for others. Why? Because I want to leave a legacy for my children.

Do you see how digging deeper can help you tap into what you truly want and why?

So what do *you* want most right now? What do *you* want to see happen in the future? What are *your* visions and dreams for your life? Now, why do you want those things? How will they make life better? What benefits—emotional, mental, and spiritual—will you receive if you reach your goals? How do you want to feel, and why?

Consider these questions too:

> What new things must happen in order for me to meet my goals?

> What changes do I need to implement in my everyday life to start putting my desires at the top of my priority list?

> What has kept me from moving forward, and how can I avoid letting it stand in the way in the future?

Plan for It

First, if you've realized that self-defeating thoughts are keeping you from living your best life with confidence, courage, and enthusiasm, make a list of those thoughts on a piece of paper or in your journal. Then try to notice when those thoughts invade your mind.

Ask God to help you live acutely aware of each time your mind is pulled back to false beliefs so you can capture those thoughts and dispute them, just as we're told to do in 2 Corinthians 10:5: "We demolish arguments and every pretension that sets itself up against the knowledge of God, and we take captive every thought to make it obedient to Christ" (NIV). Stop them in their tracks, reframe them into something positive, and you'll be on your way to changing your patterns of thinking once and for all. This practice can help you completely transform the way you think, feel, and live every single day. Make it a priority to focus each day on how precious you are to Him, and gradually you'll begin to see yourself through His eyes instead of merely your own.

Act on It

Take your answers to all the questions above, and start thinking about what goals you need to set to begin turning your deepest desires into realities. Put on your goal-setting cap, and get ready to draft a blueprint for the next chapter of building the life you want to live! Without using any specific format, simply put on paper what you want to achieve. Dream big and think outside the box, but also include the small goals you hope to achieve along the way. Every goal, big or small, is important. Make your list of goals with the expectation that the impossible is possible.

Reread the ten strategies for learning to trust that your future is in God's hands. Then, write those ten strategies in your journal, and jot down ideas for how you can implement each of them to begin giving birth to your new beginning. A solid plan is the foundation for success.

Pray over It

Lord, I pray for Your supernatural intervention; help me capture my negative and self-defeating thoughts. Help me learn to be my own best friend. Help me build confidence and courage because my identity lies in You. I commit to trusting that You have my future already divinely orchestrated and to seeking Your guidance as I set goals for the life I want to create. I commit to leaning on You and to stop letting doubts and negativity stand in my way. Please help me stay motivated and excited about the possibilities I can embrace if I put all my trust in You. Amen.

Write your own prayer to Jesus in this space.

Chapter 9

Time to Start Planning

I once attended a Major League Baseball game at Camden Yards in Baltimore. Shortly after arriving, I noticed a young man down in front of me making a spectacle of himself. Rather than wearing the standard favorite team sportswear, he had on nothing but a swimsuit, tennis shoes, and a long, striped beach towel tied around his neck, with two large words written across the towel in black Sharpie: "WAVE MAN."

He was quite entertaining as he jumped up and down, running back and forth from section to section, relentlessly trying to get the crowds to do the wave, where people stand and raise their arms in one seating section after another.

He started this challenge at the very beginning of the first inning and put forth unbelievable effort to meet his goal. But after a couple of hours, my friends and I went from being entertained and enthralled by him to feeling sorry for him as his efforts to build the wave seemed completely futile. We all began to hope he would give up and sit down to avoid any further humiliation.

But instead of giving up, he got creative, using every means he could think of to get the wave started in that huge stadium. He even began strategically positioning friends at different spots around the venue and then calling them on their cell phones when the wave was getting close to them so they could run around and elicit the wave from their respective sections.

Then to our surprise, in the ninth inning when the game was almost over, his hard work paid off! We all sat in awe as we watched tens of thousands of people stand up and do the wave around the entire Camden Yards stadium—and not only once but nine times!

This one individual, who was unknown and unimportant to the whole scheme of the ball game, was able to get thousands of people to listen to him and follow his lead! He had set a goal, and he wasn't going to let up until he achieved it. He had a vision for how awesome it would be if he was successful, and his determination and perseverance paid off. He inspired me so much I've never forgotten it.

I witnessed over several hours how one person who followed his dream for making something happen, which essentially should have been impossible, experienced that dream coming true right before his eyes. His fantasy became reality. If one person can influence more than forty thousand people to do something they hadn't planned on doing, even if it's something as silly as the wave, consider what might happen in your own life if you set solid goals for yourself, commit to persevering no matter how long it takes, and refuse to give up until those dreams become a reality!

If you want change, it requires taking action. And then you keep going. And going.

If you have a dream for your life that doesn't seem to be coming true or that even feels impossible, it doesn't mean that your dream isn't meant for you or that it won't or can't happen.

It doesn't mean that you're not worthy of pursuing and creating the changes you long for, in yourself and your life. It doesn't mean that you're not talented enough or that God doesn't have wonderful plans to open doors for you and unfold a fabulous future. It doesn't mean that you heard Him wrong about that longing in your spirit. It doesn't mean that you're too young or too old and you missed your window of opportunity.

It simply means that whatever you've been doing so far isn't getting you the outcome you desire. You've probably heard that old saying: "The definition of insanity is continuing to do the same thing over and over but expecting a different result." I also heard this saying recently: "The stew is always going to taste the same if you never change the recipe."

Both statements remind us that the only way to invite positive changes into our lives is to do something that we haven't been doing before. Either we grow, or we stay the same. Plus, we should never give up when we go through one bad chapter or when things aren't happening in our timing, because our stories don't end there.

If you want to see a different outcome and you're longing to kick off your new beginning with excitement, enthusiasm, and optimism, your thoughts as well as your actions must be different first.

Prior to moving into ministry years ago, I spent fifteen years working in the corporate world. During those years, I learned a lot of lessons, had some successes and failures, and developed a variety of skills that I still use today in different capacities. But one of the most important things I ever learned was that goal setting is essential in every aspect of life.

In the role I held as the Southeast operations services manager at a Big Four accounting firm, I was required annually to set dozens of personal-development, performance, and job-related goals.

Since I would have to account for my progress or the lack thereof at the end of the year, I knew I needed a strategy for keeping up with everything and keeping myself on track. I wanted to have tangible proof of the goals I had met and the areas I needed to continue focusing on. So I created a goal-setting binder using three simple steps:

1. I made a list of all the SMART (specific, measurable, action oriented, realistic, and time bound[1]—we'll delve into this more in a moment!) goals and sub-objectives I wanted and needed to meet that year. Those things my supervisor expected of me, important responsibilities related to my position, and personal goals for myself.

2. I typed up each goal on a separate sheet of paper, printed them all out, and put them together in a three-ring binder with a tab for each goal.

3. Each time I met one of my goals or each time I met a short-term sub-objective that took me closer to meeting that goal, I made note of it in my binder in the appropriate section, or I printed out the relevant documentation and inserted it into the binder.

At the end of the year, as I completed my performance review and wrote down my progress, accomplishments, and successes for the previous twelve months, I had an invaluable tool right at my fingertips with tons of pertinent information.

I was able to look back at every big and little thing I had done throughout the year in multiple areas of my job and personal life, many of which I would have completely forgotten had I not kept such good records. And for the goals I hadn't fulfilled yet, I at least had concrete evidence of all the things I had done in support of those goals. Even though I still had some work to do, I could see and celebrate my progress and adjust anything that needed tweaking.

That goal-setting regimen was for a professional position, but it helped me understand that setting goals, or dream casting, for our personal lives is a must. Just like a builder can't be successful in building a house without a blueprint, we can't effectively work toward making our dreams and desires for new beginnings—or a brighter future—come true if we don't have our specific goals outlined, with a solid action plan in place to meet them. If we can dream it, we can do it, but we must plan for it. Progress always begins with planning.

Make a Declaration, Not a Resolution

After she read an article in *Fast Company* magazine about the 1953 Yale study of goals, Gail Matthews, a professor in the Dominican University of California's department of psychology, became interested in the study of procrastination. According to the article, the Yale study is an urban legend, but its premise is said to be that people who write down their specific goals and dreams for their future are far more likely to be successful than those who don't write them down or maybe don't set any goals at all. So in 2015, she decided to do a study of her own. She recruited 267 participants to be a part of her study, which focused on how the achievement of goals is strongly influenced by writing them down, creating an action plan for each one, and having someone hold you accountable for acting on those aspirations and persevering.

The study showed that more than 75 percent of people who wrote their goals down, created an action plan for each one, and sent weekly updates to a friend reported that they either had met their goals or were at least halfway there, compared with only 35 percent of people who had just thought about their goals and didn't write them down, kept them to themselves, and had no accountability partner or friend to support and push them.

Matthews said, "My study provides empirical evidence for the effectiveness of three coaching tools: accountability, commitment, and writing down one's goals."[2]

Goal setting isn't generally deemed the most exciting topic to talk about. I get it. And typically the only time people are committed to goal setting is when a new year rolls around and they get excited about calling them New Year's resolutions. A new year brings a level of anticipation about starting again on something we didn't succeed at the year before or starting something new that we feel will improve our lives. But unfortunately, the success rate for sticking with those resolutions is low.

About 44 percent of Americans make a New Year's resolution before the last day of the year is over. Only 31 percent stick with the promises they made to themselves the prior year, and 81 percent have fallen off track with their New Year's goals by February.[3]

Get the picture? All those desires of your heart for change, for your dreams to come true, and to begin again with passion and excitement most likely won't ever happen if you don't invest time and effort in writing down what you want most and then creating an action plan to make it become a reality.

A resolution is defined as "the act of resolving or determining upon an action, course of action, method, procedure, etc.; a resolve; a decision or determination; the mental state or quality of being resolved or resolute; firmness of purpose."[4] But a declaration is "the act of declaring; announcement; a positive, explicit, or formal statement; proclamation; something that is announced, avowed, or proclaimed."[5]

Which one sounds more empowering to you? A declaration, of course! You're not only resolving to try to meet your desires or deciding you want to make something happen, and then if it does, it does, and if it doesn't, it doesn't. Instead, you're declaring to yourself once and for all that you will make things different going forward. You're proclaiming to yourself that you won't stop until you achieve your desires, and that is powerful.

The best way to develop and clarify your declarations and make plans that will drive your future in the direction you want it to go is to use the SMART goals formula, which was developed by George Doran (along with Arthur Miller and James Cunningham) in a 1981 article.[6]

SMART is an acronym for five crucial components that every goal needs:

> S—specific (simple, sensible, significant)
> M—measurable (having a tangible way to track your progress)
> A—action oriented (including concrete steps to propel you forward)
> R—realistic (relevant to your life, reasonable, attainable)
> T—time bound (involving a specific time for when to have met your goal)

No matter how long it takes to start making headway on your goals, trust that something is always growing from your struggles and pursuits. That something is *you*. Remember what I said earlier: we must do the work for God to bless the work.

Doran, Miller, and Cunningham strongly believed that setting goals adds value to what you're doing, allows you to assess your progress along the way, and helps you determine how to overcome hurdles, manage your time effectively, and set measures for success. All of which becomes your inspiration when the going gets tough, especially on those bad days when you don't think you can ever move out of your comfort zone. We all need motivation, and planning is a must.

So I'm going to get off my soapbox about goal setting so you can get down to business. You've got this because God's got you, sweet friend, and this process—as tedious as it might seem—can make or break your success at beginning again. I pray you believe in yourself enough and have enough faith in your capabilities and in God to trust that if He planted a dream in your heart of how you want things to be, He will help you bring it to fruition.

The act of setting SMART goals simply means knowing what your goals are and breaking them down into manageable chunks. A lofty goal or a God-sized dream can feel overwhelming. Hopelessness that life can ever be different can keep you trapped in your current state. In fact, the sheer thought of trying to follow through on your declarations can cause mental paralysis and confusion. This process can help you avoid that.

Breaking our small and big long-term goals down into short-term objectives makes those lofty accomplishments and fantasies we long for—and anything attached to our successful *beginning again*—seem much less intimidating and much more attainable, simply because we can see the steps we need to take more clearly and we have a plan for achieving them. In planning for our future, we gain confidence for our future.

You see, the act of goal setting, this declaration-making process, allows us to see increments of progress to aim for. It prevents us from getting frustrated and discouraged as easily, because when we see any signs of development or progress, we'll be more energized to keep taking that next step. And great things happen when a lot of small things get done well every day.

I bet if you and I could sit down over coffee and talk freely about the dreams and desires in your heart, you wouldn't have any problem listing out all the things you want to accomplish, the changes you want to make or see happen, who you want to be, and what you want to do to kick off your new beginning. You already know how you want life to be different, and I bet your wishes would easily roll off your tongue while we sipped coffee and fellowshipped. I also imagine you telling me all that with a sparkle of enthusiasm in your eyes!

But since you and I can't meet in person, let's just pretend we're hanging out in your favorite coffee shop, with our favorite lattes and cinnamon buns, enjoying the aroma of coffee wafting through the air on a wintry day amid the buzz of conversation from the other customers. You pull out a little notepad, and we start chatting. I ask you to spill all your hopes and dreams, those ideas that make your heart skip a beat at the thought of them. What would your life look like if you had the power to change anything? Where do you want to be in a year? Five years? Ten years?

Those are the things you can begin writing on your notepad right now. Write freely about everything that comes to mind, your dreams and visions for the future, as if you were pouring your heart out to me. Don't hold back. Let them flow.

Then get a refill on your cup of coffee, and start writing every single wish, vision, dream, or fantasy as a SMART goal. To refresh your memory, make each goal specific and measurable. Include actions you'll need to start doing to begin making progress. Keep it realistic, yet dream big, and set some deadlines for yourself.

Leaning into your faith won't dissolve all your fears, but it will help you rise above them.

Let's take a moment to explore each of the elements of the SMART goals strategy in more detail.

Specific means outlining the what, why, and how of your desired goal (you should have already explored your what and why in your journal, and if so, you're already well on your way!). State exactly what your goal is, no matter how lofty it may seem. And if you've ever shared your dreams or goals with someone else and they threw cold water on them, forget that! God gave *you* your dreams, not them. If He planted a goal in your heart, it's your job to nurture it, grow it, and help it bloom. You don't have to defend or explain your decisions or declarations. It's your life, and you get only one life to live. Live it without apologies!

No matter what they are, the goals you set should be measurable so you have tangible evidence that you've accomplished the goal or you're at least making progress. Usually, the entire goal statement is a measure for the project, but there are often several short-term or smaller measurements built into the goal.

Next, outline your action plan. Simply identify the exact steps you plan to take to help you achieve success. Remember what I've stated before: Think of the things you need to start doing today to create the tomorrow you long for. Brainstorm what you'll need to do, what resources you'll need, what changes or sacrifices must be made, and so on.

Your goals should stretch you slightly so you feel challenged and need to lean into God and your faith but should be defined well enough that you can actually achieve them. We can dream big, but we should also be realistic. And we can meet most any goal we set for ourselves when we plan our course of action wisely and establish a time frame that allows us to strategically carry them out. Keep in mind that leaning into your faith won't dissolve all your fears but it will help you rise above them.

Goals should be linked to a time frame that creates a practical sense of urgency and accountability. Without deadlines, meeting the goal is unlikely to happen. Goals should measure outcomes, not just activities. When we set a time frame for completion, we stay more motivated to meet that deadline even if it's one we set for ourselves. It may sound silly to set deadlines for yourself, but if you make a declaration that you will meet them, those deadlines can become your primary inspiration to keep persevering!

As examples, here are a couple of goals I once set for myself:

- Reclaim my happiness and security after my divorce (specific and realistic) by obtaining employment by a certain date and reducing debt (measurable), journaling, keeping family close, staying grounded in my faith (action oriented), and feeling secure and independent by a specific date (time bound).

- Build a successful coaching business for aspiring authors (specific and realistic) through strategic preparation and multiple marketing strategies (action oriented) by a specific date (time bound) with quarterly checks on progress (measurable).

I obviously had to reach lots of smaller subgoals as I worked toward my ultimate goals, but each small step got me closer to where I wanted to be.

Just as important as setting SMART goals is having a process to review them. If we don't have a way to track progress and stay motivated to work toward any goal we're striving for, it's highly unlikely we'll stay on track and highly likely we'll get discouraged and quit, falling into the same category as the people who break New Year's resolutions. The goal-setting binder I mentioned earlier can be a great tool, so consider making one of your own, or you can come up with any system that will work well for you to stay organized and goal focused.

The Four Cs

We also need to consider four important factors when we get serious about working toward making our dreams come true in our seasons of new beginnings. I call them the four Cs.

1. **Curiosity:** Be willing to dream big. Imagine yourself and how you will feel if what you want to change actually happens. Allow yourself to be curious about all the possibilities of a happy new beginning and get excited about it. Ponder what needs to change and

what you need to do for your visions of the future to come true.

2. **Courage:** Remember those twenty seconds of insane courage? They're inside you too! They're not only for major acts of bravery but also for smaller things that feel outside your comfort zone—including getting serious about goals. We may not always feel strong, but we can always be brave. Courage doesn't mean we don't feel afraid or discouraged; it just means we don't let that fear and discouragement stop us.

3. **Confidence:** Have confidence in yourself and your gifts. Remember those lists you made in chapter 6 of your positive traits and the accomplishments you're most proud of? Let those lists be your motivator and the mirror in which you see yourself as the amazing person God created you to be. Shed the idea of perfectionism, and acknowledge your gain and not just your gaps. Don't look at where you are now and allow a lack of confidence to cause you to begin assuming things can't change. Instead, be confident! Identify your strengths and skills and how they can serve you well; then set your sights on where you want to be and what you need to do to get there.

4. **Community:** Surround yourself with people who support you and believe in you, as well as people who are like you. Fear and lack of confidence are contagious, and so are courage and success, so choose your friends wisely. Consider whether you need to prune

> your inner circle and whether there is someone who
> won't be supportive of your visions for a new begin-
> ning and a new you. If your inner circle doesn't
> understand or believe in your dreams and desires,
> they won't help you or hold you accountable for
> working toward achieving them. Don't let someone
> else's disbelief cause you to lose belief in yourself.

Not only does life dictate that we need goals, but Scripture supports this concept as well. Consider Proverbs 21:5: "Good planning and hard work lead to prosperity, but hasty shortcuts lead to poverty." *The Message* words that verse this way: "Careful planning puts you ahead in the long run; hurry and scurry puts you further behind." This verse suggests that goal setting is not only encouraged by God but also absolutely necessary if we want to be successful in doing the things He has nudged us to do or pursuing the dreams He has given us.

Then in Psalm 37:3 we read, "Trust in the LORD and do good; live in the land and cultivate faithfulness" (NASB). This verse reminds us to trust the Lord with our plans and to always focus on His faithfulness during the journey. And then most importantly, Proverbs 16:3 says, "Commit your actions to the LORD, and your plans will succeed." This verse provides reassurance that God cares about our hopes and dreams for our new beginnings and that although success is never guaranteed in the way we may have in mind, we can find peace in knowing we have God on our side and He is leading the way.

All throughout the Bible we see examples of God directly leading people to set goals for what they believed He had called them to do and pursue them by faith. Esther having the goal of saving her people. David having the goal of defeating the giant. Moses having the goal of reaching the Promised Land. These three, as well as countless others who followed callings that seemed beyond their capabilities, make it clear that Scripture encourages us to set goals that align with God's will for us and to follow through on them.

Last, let's look at Psalm 37:5: "Commit your way to the LORD, trust also in Him, and He shall bring it to pass" (NKJV). Here we find hope that God can bring our goals and dreams to fulfillment and that we are the vessel to make them happen.

It's okay to want more for yourself. It's okay to long for a better present and future. It's okay to draw those wishes out of your heart and set goals for yourself and your life. It's better than okay to work hard to achieve those goals and be proud of your progress.

The time you spend doing so will be time well spent. Goals force us to contemplate what we truly want and lean on God for direction and clarity. They help us break down what it will take to get what we want into doable action items. Goals give us focus. Goals help us measure progress, so even if we're not where we want to be yet, we can see how we've made strides in the right direction and are further along than when we started. Knowing we're making strides helps us stay motivated to overcome procrastination, keep being persistent, and hold firm to your purpose of kick-starting your new beginning.

And when we achieve a goal, we get a little taste of victory. And that is a sweet, sweet taste that will boost your spirit and fill you with the desire to taste it again and again.

We will all stumble along the way, but never doubt you've got this, because God's got you. Your success is up to you, and your faith is what fuels your success in reaching your goals. I read this quote once: "Faith it until you make it. Faith guarantees nothing and yet it changes every-thing."[7] It simply means that setting and pursuing goals is about faith in God and His abilities, even when we don't feel confident or equipped. What an awesome reminder that, on those days when we feel that noth-ing is happening like we want it to or that we're falling short in some way, we can at least keep leaning into our faith and trusting the Leader.

Imagine how you'll feel a year from now, five years from now, ten years from now, as you look back and remember this season when life seemed so uncertain, scary, and unsatisfying and then look at your present and see the fruits of your hard work, perseverance, and unwavering trust in Him.

You might have heard this saying by American futurist Joel Arthur Barker: "Vision without action is merely a dream. Action without vision just passes the time. Vision with action can change the world."[8] Allow yourself to have vision, and then prepare yourself to take action. Don't just think about your goals; start working toward them. Your action can change your world over time, and possibly that of others as well.

You owe it to yourself to be the best version of who God called you to be. We often tend to put everyone else first, and that's not bad. But there comes a time—especially when you face new seasons or transition periods—to finally put yourself, your dreams, your new beginning, and your future first so you can march forward in bold faith into your new life.

It's okay to dream, my friend. So dream big. Don't just set goals; view them as declarations to yourself and commitments to make your deepest desires come true. Then do the work to set yourself up for success.

Moving Forward

Think about It

If you haven't already, get out your notepad and write down all your hopes and dreams, those ideas that make your heart skip a beat at the thought of them. Write out your ideal vision of the future. What would your life look like if you had the power to change anything? Where do you want to be in a year? Five years? Ten years? Write freely about everything that comes to mind; don't hold anything back, and let your thoughts, ideas, and dreams flow. Remember the four Cs—curiosity, courage, confidence, and community—and make sure they are part of your every day.

Then write a letter to yourself. Imagine you've already accomplished the goals you have for yourself and your future. All those goals you set and worked hard to achieve have already happened. Think about how you'll feel and what life will look like. You'll be able to look back on this letter later and reminisce about how far you've come and how much you and your life have changed for the better.

Plan for It

Based on what you wrote in the above section, put your ideas into a list organized by importance and urgency. Then use the SMART goal formula shared in this chapter to begin crafting your own goals. What declarations do you want to set for yourself? Turn those declarations—those big dreams in your heart—into SMART goals. This is the most important thing you can do to help you truly begin again! Don't procrastinate—get started today! If you're a crafty person or a visual learner, create a vision board to display somewhere in your home to serve as a daily motivator and keep you striving for what you want. A vision board can be fun to make and is simply a collage of images and words, maybe taken from magazines or the internet, representing your wishes or goals, that can serve as inspiration and motivation each time you look at it.

Act on It

For each of your new SMART goals, determine every little and big action step you'll need to take to make that dream come true. Be as detail oriented as you can! Then draft a complete action plan. Think about where you are right now and what is the next thing you need to do to get on your way toward each goal. Every SMART goal should have these subgoals attached to outline what those steps are. And to help you stay excited and determined on the journey, don't forget to think of ways you can reward yourself for meeting small and lofty goals! Also, consider purchasing a three-ring binder and making your own goal-setting binder to keep track of your progress. Making goal setting a priority is a surefire way to proceed into your new beginning with a solid plan in place.

Pray over It

Lord, You know the desires of my heart and the goals I want to achieve. Help me believe in myself and my dreams and stay motivated and inspired to pursue them. Please prick my spirit if I step outside Your will for me, and help me have open eyes to see You at work in my life. I believe You want my life to be full of joy in every season. I declare today that You will do exceedingly abundantly above all that I ask for or imagine. I will look for Your blessings and trust in Your ways and Your timing. I will cling to the promise that I am surrounded by Your favor. Amen.

Write your own prayer to Jesus in this space.

Chapter 10

Time to Start Trusting

May 26, 1990: My wedding day.

May 26, 2016: My twenty-sixth wedding anniversary, which went uncelebrated for the first time because I no longer had a husband.

May 26, 2022: The day I sold our family home, which I had lived in for twenty-five years, and the day I closed on and moved into a new home.

May 26, 2023: The day I poured a cup of coffee and was reminded that God is always in the details of our lives, including the beginning and the end of seasons, and we can always trust Him.

You see, I have a spiral-bound inspirational-quote booklet that sits on my kitchen counter with a scriptural quote for each date throughout the year. As I was pouring my coffee that morning, I glanced over at the quote of the day, and the words made my heart leap:

> Today, be reminded of three things—you are stronger
> than you ever imagined, Jesus is closer than you ever
> realized, and you are loved more than you ever knew.[1]

I was reminded suddenly how God had shown me I was indeed stronger than I would have ever imagined. As I look back, there is no explanation for all I was able to get through and accomplish during the hardest season of my life, except for the intervention of my heavenly Father.

May 26, 1990, was the beginning of a new season for me as a newly married woman. May 26, 2016, was the precise end of that season. On May 26, 2022, I officially began anew. I not only closed on my new home but also closed out that chapter of living and started walking out another brand-new beginning.

Then on May 26, 2023, I recognized that Jesus was closer than I had ever realized, especially during those times when I thought He didn't see my pain and wasn't at work—those times when waiting for things to get better seemed to take forever and I wondered if He even cared. Yet I can now see His fingerprints scattered throughout every season of my life.

I smiled at the joy of knowing with my whole heart that Jesus loves me more than I can understand and certainly more than I deserve. He loves me so much that even the tiniest of details, like perfectly orchestrated dates that are significant to me, also hold significance to Him and serve as proof of His absolute, flawless, impeccable timing in all things. He loved me enough to place the perfect words my heart needed to hear in a tiny little quote book on the exact day that would allow me to see His incredible intervention in my life. And He loves you that much too.

It's often not blaring signs that show us proof of God's work in our lives but coincidental details where there is no other explanation but God.

These details birth our motivation for new beginnings. I've stressed over and over in this book the importance of walking in faith and remembering God's past faithfulness as we do so. We've seen what He can do and how much He loves us, and we can put our faith and trust in Him, knowing He already has our next seasons planned out.

Faith that God has our future in His hands will help us keep going when the going gets tough. When we wonder if we can survive. When we doubt if things will ever change. If we'll be happy again. If we can do that big thing that seems out of reach. If we'll succeed at achieving the dreams God has placed in our hearts and overcoming the challenges that lie ahead, or if we'll fail miserably and fall flat on our faces instead.

I had all those thoughts and many more, and maybe you do too. I've struggled with those types of thoughts in more than one season of life. Walking boldly into the unknown, even with faith on our side, feels scary and uncomfortable. Taking a chance on ourselves, our dreams, and our desires for new beginnings and fresh hope pushes us out of our comfort zone. But you know what? Incredible things can happen when we're willing to take a chance on ourselves and our God. In fact, making ourselves uncomfortable is the quickest way to start becoming that person we long to be.

God has pushed me out of my comfort zone more times than I can count, and every single time, He has shown me how faith changes things and opens the door for Him to do something in me, through me, and for me that I would never experience otherwise.

Faith Stretching Is a Good Thing

Many years ago, I had an experience in which God pushed me out of my comfort zone further than ever before. I had signed up with my family to participate in a mission trip in another state, where we would renovate homes of needy families. Little did I know that God planned to stretch me far beyond what was comfortable.

I wasn't stretched as I climbed up a ten-foot ladder to hand someone a heavy can of paint. I wasn't stretched as I sprawled across my noisy, uncomfortable air mattress every night on the hard floor of an old high school, hoping it wouldn't completely deflate before I woke up. I wasn't stretched as I endured 105-degree temperatures in the southern heat of summer while wearing the required attire of thick cotton T-shirts and full-length blue jeans that stuck to my sweaty legs like glue.

I wasn't even stretched when I took showers near total strangers, with only a thin curtain between us, or when I shared said awkward shower with a large, dead, winged creature lying in the drain and a spiderweb hanging overhead.

None of these things were enjoyable or comfortable, but they weren't really outside my comfort zone. Yet when it came time to walk through the local neighborhood, knock on doors, and share the gospel with strangers, with the looming fear that a door might be slammed in my face, or worse, I felt my faith being stretched. Looking back now, I can see that God was pushing me, once again, into a faith zone outside the mental boundaries where I felt secure. I was confronted with the decision either to stretch my faith or to play it safe. In other words, I had to decide to put my faith in God and trust in His plans, even when I had no idea what was going to happen.

I could have easily sent my work crew down the street without me and remained standing in the shade of the big oak trees while the others on the team approached the homeowners with holy confidence. But God had planted a burning conviction in my heart to trust Him and do some serious stretching. As it turned out, I was the one who received the greatest blessing in doing so.

There are countless stories in the Bible of God calling people to leave their comfortable places, and with each one, we see how the stretching of their faith brought blessings they never imagined.

Abraham trusted God for the child he was promised, despite his and his wife's age. His faith-stretching ended with him holding a little baby named Isaac.

The disciples feared for their lives when a violent storm threatened to sink their boat, but Peter's faith to step out of the boat resulted in him seeing Jesus do a miracle as his human feet walked on water.

Jesus told a crippled man whose muscles were atrophied to get up and walk. The man stretched his faith as he stretched out his legs and walked for the very first time.

A blind man had the faith to believe Jesus could heal his eyes, and within seconds, he saw Jesus face to face with those very eyes.

Joshua may have felt ridiculous walking around the walls of Jericho for seven days, but he stretched his faith and eventually saw the walls come crumbling down.

Joseph's faith was stretched during the years he spent in a dark dungeon, but it was that very faith that landed him in the throne room as second only to Pharaoh.

Esther stretched her faith and even risked her life when she chose to breach royal protocol, approach the king without being summoned, and ask him to spare the Jews. As a result, the Jewish people were saved, and she created a legacy.

It seems crazy now to look back and recall how utterly stressed and frantic I was about talking to someone about Jesus on that mission trip. I think my heart was racing a hundred miles an hour and my sweating from stress was worse than my perspiration from the heat.

But obedience always leads to blessings, and I had the blessing of being a blessing.

The sweet people we met were at first hesitant to talk to us, as we all would be if strangers showed up on our doorstep. However, after a few simple questions and some chitchat, they were honored we were taking time to care about them and ask how we could pray for them. I met beautiful women and precious children, all of whom simply needed to know they mattered to someone and they were seen.

They were cared about. They were prayed for. They were blessed. And so was I.

God calls us all to do some faith-stretching every now and then, and often that stretching comes in seasons of new beginnings.

Whether we're called to do something new that God has impressed on our hearts, big or small, or called to trust Him during a difficult or transitional season full of unknowns, He always rewards faith-stretching with wonderful blessings.

Maybe you feel like God is stretching you too much right now. Or maybe you want to be bold, but you feel hesitant to get started or confused about how to do so. But in all honesty, we have no choice but to change with the changing seasons of life, and we can't try to stretch a season into a lifetime. In addition, if what we're doing doesn't stretch us a little, is it even worth doing?

God always wants to stretch us, yet He will never stretch us beyond what we're capable of in Him. When we're willing to be stretched and push ourselves to do hard things, we will eventually see change happen— in us and around us.

Sometimes a little faith stretching is the very best thing we can do for ourselves, our new beginnings, and our future.

God's Sweet Surprises Are Endless

After my divorce, I had no choice but to figure out how to begin again on my own and learn how to transition from married to single. I also went from financially stable to desperately broke and trying to find a full-time job for the first time in fifteen years to provide for myself and my children. Shortly after that, I transitioned from forty something to fifty years old. (Come on—milestone birthdays are big, emotional transitions too!) Then I went from full-time mom to empty nester.

I went through so many transitions, forced to begin again in so many areas of my life, all the while in a state of grief and fear, that it just didn't seem fair. Yet God gave me strength I didn't know I had, along with courage and confidence I had never experienced before. He provided in ways that left me in awe. And He brought me to where I am today, and I didn't even know it was where I longed to be.

Then last year, I experienced yet another God-incidence, proving once again that God is always orchestrating the details of our lives, including new beginnings. I realized how He had been at work in ways I could never have predicted, and I was amazed yet again at His supernatural, incredible planning and divinely orchestrated timing.

As a writer myself and someone who has coached writers for years through my full-time job, God had instilled in me a passion to work with aspiring authors on a more personal level. I wanted to help other people get their God-stories on paper and into the hands of readers whose lives could be changed by their written words.

So, albeit with hesitation, I set my sights on starting my own author coaching business, mapped out all my SMART goals, and put all my energy into making that dream come true. I spent months and months working on my website, developing my service offerings, writing content, getting new photos made, and doing all the things launching a new business entails. I'm a master at "doing."

But when it came time to promote my new venture, I procrastinated. I'm apparently also a master at finding reasons to put off doing something new when I am unsure how it's going to turn out.

I worried about not getting any clients once I launched. Who was I to think people would want me to teach them about writing? How would I even find writers to work with me without a lofty marketing budget? I worried about overcommitting myself. I already worked a full-time job on top of writing this book under a looming deadline. What if I did get a few clients but then couldn't handle the workload or find sufficient time to do it all? I fretted over the money I had spent on my website and doubted my decisions. What if I had heard God wrong and this wasn't really His calling for me?

What if trying to create a new beginning in my new season wasn't really what God had intended? So many what-ifs!

I found every reason possible to not launch this business I had been working so diligently on. The business I had originally believed to be God's nudging on my heart now felt like a huge blind—and maybe dumb—leap of faith. The courage that had fueled this dream seemed to be a thing of the past, and my confidence waned. I was being stretched yet again to take a chance on God and myself and push past the doubts, insecurities, and fears that kept invading my thoughts.

Eventually, the day came when I knew I had to stop procrastinating, making excuses, and giving in to fear. I had a little chat with myself and decided I didn't want to stay stuck in analysis paralysis forever. I had to choose whether to trust God with this new adventure—this new beginning—or sit idly by and let my dreams die. I knew it was time to begin and spread the word about my business, so I typed up the email and reviewed it again and again for accuracy (you know, still finding ways to procrastinate).

As my fingers hovered nervously over the keyboard, I finally closed my eyes, took a deep breath, and hit the Send button. And off it went to tens of thousands of blog subscribers. No retracting it.

Anxiety flooded over me—what had I just done? Yikes. However, my apprehension was quickly interrupted by a quiet voice in my spirit.

What is today's date, Tracie? God whispered.

Huh? Perplexed by this random thought, I glanced over at the calendar and was taken aback. It wasn't until that very moment that I realized the significance of the date. Yet another clear-as-a-bell God-incidence. The very reason God had prompted my heart to check the calendar.

I realized it was exactly seven years to the day from when my twenty-five-year marriage had imploded and my entire life had been turned upside down. Yet again, impeccable timing that gave me literal chill bumps.

My mind replayed a vision of the unforgettable, traumatic day that had brought me to my knees exactly seven years ago. I couldn't even believe it had been seven years, when in some ways it seemed to have happened yesterday. But God quickly shifted my thoughts and helped me refocus.

Rather than holding memories of heartache and fear, now this exact date on the calendar would hold a fresh, new meaning. It was now a God-ordained, divinely orchestrated date that would live on in my heart forever.

God immediately calmed my anxiety and gently reminded me that, over the past seven years, He had turned my life around completely, exchanged my sadness for joy, and performed more miracles than I could count. He had helped me meet goals I never thought I could accomplish.

I certainly hadn't planned on kicking off my risky new business project on this particular day—I hadn't chosen any specific date to launch the project at all. So at first I thought to myself, *It just happened.*

But did it?

A smile crept across my face and tears formed in my eyes as I saw God with great clarity amid all the messy details of my life.

And now, in His perfect, miraculous timing, He had brought me to a place I never thought I would find myself—healed, restored, whole, and filled with passion for a purpose I never imagined all those years ago. He reminded me that He has our future in His hands. And it is good. He turns pain into purpose and sorrow into joy.

I immediately recalled how, in Scripture, the number seven often symbolizes a sense of fullness or completeness. In fact, from one end of the Bible to the other, from Genesis to Revelation, the number seven appears 735 times and often refers to the holy works of God, repeatedly serving as proof of the perfection and beauty He orchestrated over and over again.

I'm certainly not complete as a person, and God still has plenty of work to do in me. But this little miracle showed me how He had brought my pain full circle to completion. He had taken what the Devil meant for evil, which I thought was the end of my life and my ministry, and turned it into something whole, new, fresh, and good.

God's work and timing are always perfect.

In Ecclesiastes 3:11, we read, "He has made everything beautiful in its time" (NIV). This verse reminds us that all things are crafted by God—including time. He is behind the way all things are and the way they will turn out. It also reminds us that everything happens exactly when it should. Not by chance or irony, but by a divine plan beyond our comprehension.

What we see as a new beginning is actually God's plan for us *from the beginning.*

Trusting God when the future seems hazy is the best thing we can do for ourselves.

As ordained by God, on the exact day I had experienced a devastating heartbreak that I thought I'd never recover from, I chose to be brave, pushed past my fear and insecurities, overcame procrastination, shifted my thoughts to things that were good rather than let the lies of the Enemy be a stumbling block, and pursued a dream. It was the birth of one of many new beginnings.

God taught me right then and there that we can't wait until we have every detail figured out or until we don't have any fear or trepidation. We must start moving toward what our hearts are telling us, and our vision will evolve out of our obedience. I read once that "if you wait for perfect conditions, you'll waste your best years in a waiting room."[2] Let's not get stuck in the waiting room of life, and remember, we can count on Jesus when we need Him most. Every time we act despite our fear, we dilute its power against us.

I love that Jesus tells us in Matthew 10:30 that "the very hairs of your head are all numbered." God takes infinite interest in even the most intimate details of our lives. There is nothing too small or trivial for Him to notice or plan.

I had no idea this was the day God had ordained to prompt me to take this leap of faith, but it was certainly not a coincidence. It was planned long before my time on earth even began. My faith soared, and this evidence of sovereignty reminded me to put all my trust in Him for all things. Always.

Why?

Nothing is ever random with God.

He had been divinely orchestrating behind the scenes to turn my ashes into beauty, in His timing, exactly and perfectly, significantly, seven years later as a symbol of the journey He had been on with me.

I'm not special and didn't get special favor. God's favor is meant for all of us, and He has perfectly planned out your life in a way only He can. You may not be able to see it now, but you can trust He is in the details. Believe with all your heart that one day you'll see His perfect plan fall into place for you too, and I promise it will cause your heart to swell and your faith to soar.

Maybe your new beginning feels scary. I get it. Scary is uncomfortable. Nobody likes to leave their comfort zone, but nothing amazing happens in comfort zones.

Stepping outside our seemingly safe places doesn't mean we intentionally throw ourselves into highly uncomfortable or difficult situations. It just means we're willing to try new things, face uncertainties with confidence and faith, embrace seasons of transitions, and take a chance on new beginnings, even during difficult situations. It means we trust our faith over our fears. Trusting God when the future seems hazy is the best thing we can do for ourselves.

Anything new will always feel a little uncomfortable because when we embrace the *new*, we're leaving our old comfort zone behind. But our heavenly Father can do His best work in the *new*. Jesus is the author of new beginnings, no matter what we're facing. In Him, we can all begin again.

Moving Forward

Think about It

How have you seen God divinely orchestrate events or seasons in your life? Ask Him to bring to mind things you may have forgotten that have shaped who you are today, and pray for the ability to see, maybe for the first time, the miraculous perfection of how He plans your life down to the smallest of details.

Plan for It

Commit to spending time in God's Word daily. Ask Him to illuminate the Scriptures that can speak directly to the feelings and transition season you are experiencing right now. Ask for peace during the waiting period. Good things always take time. Give God a chance to show you the way.

Act on It

Make a timeline of major events in your life, including dates, people, good and bad experiences, and other important information. This may take some time and is likely not a task you can do in one sitting. In doing so, you'll begin painting the picture of the masterpiece God has been working on in your life. Let the proof of His miracles be the foundation of trusting Him with your future. Don't be disappointed if you don't see the masterpiece right away. God didn't build your life in one day, and it takes time to see what He has been working on.

Pray over It

Lord, please bring to memory all the ways You've been precisely coordinating the details of my life. Help me trust You in all things going forward and finally start feeling confident that I can do the things burning in my heart and that I have what it takes to make change happen. I want to feel fully confident in myself and my abilities, all because You created me and You created me for good things. Amen.

Write your own prayer to Jesus in this space.

Chapter 11

Time to Say Goodbye to What Was

We've all had to say goodbye before. And goodbyes are never fun, except those ones where we can say, "This isn't goodbye, just see ya later." But all too often there is no "see ya later" when we must bid farewell to a season.

Letting go of the past and saying goodbye to the life you once had can be painful, but it's necessary. We need closure on every season, whether it's a long one or a short one. We need closure so we can transition to where God wants us to be, rather than mentally stay stuck where we used to be.

A goodbye can seem hard because essentially it's an end to something. Some part of our lives that will never be the same again. But when it comes to accepting the reality that our lives have changed and our future is going to look different from what we once thought it would, getting closure is necessary.

How do we do that? And most importantly, how do we do that well? We don't want to let our past weigh down our future and keep us from accepting and embracing change, but what if it's just too darn hard to let go? I understand entirely.

However, I've learned that we grow when we let go. And sometimes, if not always, we have to let go of what we thought the present and the future would look like and learn to find joy in the story we're living and the story God is writing for our future.

On that God-ordained day when I moved out of my family home, I had to say one last goodbye. I asked the new owners to wait outside while I took one last walk around the house alone. They respectfully agreed, so I turned on the video on my phone, opened the squeaky garage door I had walked through thousands of times, and went inside.

I stood in the kitchen for a minute and scanned the room, allowing my mind to revisit memories I hadn't thought about for quite some time. I could almost see my little ones dancing in the kitchen, eating their Pop-Tarts, sitting on the countertops pressing snowman-shaped cookie cutters into homemade dough, helping me cook as they grew older, sharing how their school days went, crying about lost first loves and school drama.

I then walked slowly from room to room, capturing every empty room on my video. No more furniture. No more piles of shoes on the stairs. No more messy rooms. No more photos on the walls, vacation souvenirs, or closets full of too many clothes. No evidence we ever even lived there.

The hollowness of the house echoed in my spirit, while my head spun with recollections of the sights, smells, and sounds that had filled the home for years. But as I turned and walked out of each room, I quietly whispered goodbye.

I even went out on my deck and said, "Goodbye, beautiful gardenia bushes, my old friends." The gardenias had all grown from one-gallon pots to seven-foot-tall bushes and blessed me with hundreds of sweet-smelling blooms every June.

I know it was just a brick-and-mortar house and we aren't supposed to get hung up on worldly, material things. And you may think I'm sounding a little crazy right about now. But it had been a huge part of my life and my heart. My ex-husband and I had built that house just for us, and to put it honestly, that house had built me and built my family. But now I had to let it go and trust God's plans for me and my future, and to do so, it was time to say goodbye.

As silly as it sounds, saying goodbye in that special way helped me have closure and freed up my heart, mind, and spirit to leave the past behind and get ready to walk through the brand-new open door God had blessed me with, literally and figuratively.

I've carried out that practice of closure many times, although each season of goodbye looked a little different. I'll spare you the long list of times when I needed closure to let go of the past and embrace what was to come, but they were all hard events in their own way, and God got me through each one. And practicing some form of saying goodbye, whether it was by simply praying or by doing something physically, played a role in helping me continue to persevere, hold my head high, set my sights on new things, accept the reality of what God was allowing, and believe He had good things in store.

Honoring the past, rather than mourning the losses, is how we can say goodbye well when transitioning from one phase of life to another or accepting changes we never wanted. It's also important when we're intentionally making changes or pursuing dreams and leaving behind things we once loved. Even good changes can be hard at times, and it's always hard to say goodbye to yesterday.

In any case, regardless of circumstance, closure is always good. And you know closure is complete when you finally feel free to take chances on embracing the new things God has in store for you.

That precious moment—in between where you once were and who you once were and where you're going and who you want to become—is the perfect place to trust God and His plans for you and your future.

Whatever transitional period you find yourself in right now, my prayer is that just maybe you're finally ready to say your goodbyes, honor what was, and embrace what is to come with open arms.

Goodbyes Require Hope

How do we say goodbye? The best way I've found is to say it with hope. Hope can transform every goodbye from the heartbreaking end of something into a positive new beginning. Romans 5:5 reminds us of this truth: "This hope will not lead to disappointment. For we know how dearly God loves us, because he has given us the Holy Spirit to fill our hearts with his love."

You can be certain your new season will bring new challenges and new growth opportunities. Say goodbye to the past, get closure in whatever way you need to, and choose to be brave so you can enter the new season God has for you with open eyes, an expectant heart, a spirit of hope, and a heart full of peace, knowing He has already gone before you.

I've shared a lot of tips thus far about how to make headway toward your goals, even in the face of difficult transitions. And though I know firsthand it can be challenging, saying goodbye to the past plays a crucial role in embracing the future God has planned for you.

Here are a few tips to tuck into your heart to help you navigate this important part of the process so you can focus your energy on beginning again with the right mindset:

1. **Let go of the past.** Accept that the past is behind you and that you can't change it or get it back. Acknowledge that not letting go, or not saying goodbye and meaning it, will keep you stuck right where you are, physically, emotionally, mentally, and even spiritually. Change is normal. Letting go of what once was and accepting what can be is necessary.

2. **Embrace your emotions.** Allow yourself to feel the emotions associated with the past. Whether it's sadness, regret, anger, or any other feeling, acknowledge and process that emotion. It's essential to give yourself permission to grieve and heal from any pain or disappointment. Having positive emotions or mixed emotions? It's okay! Allow yourself to feel good about the changes you have coming, even if other people don't understand. This is your life. You do what's best for you.

3. **Give yourself closure.** Think about what you need to have closure on. A relationship? A death? A major life change? A pet? A financial crunch? Health? Whatever it is that is robbing you of joy and keeping you from forging ahead, pray about how to give yourself closure in that area. Nothing is too silly or

trivial. Don't worry about what anyone else thinks. Again, this is your life. Your heart. Your past and future. Do whatever it takes to cleanse your heart and mind and free yourself up for God's new, which is His best for you.

4. **Practice forgiveness.** Forgiveness is a powerful tool for letting go. If you're like me, forgiveness might feel like you're letting people off the hook even though they were responsible for thrusting you into difficult transitions. But forgiving those who have hurt you and letting go of bitterness isn't about condoning their actions. It's about freeing yourself up for the good things God has in store. Need to forgive yourself? Love yourself enough to do that too, because God has already given you that gift.

5. **View the past through a positive lens.** Reflect on the lessons and wisdom you gained from your experiences rather than focusing on mistakes or regrets. Remember, you aren't starting over from scratch or beginning again with nothing under your belt. You have a lifetime of knowledge, seasoning, training, and practice at doing the hard things. Recognize how your experiences have shaped you and fostered personal growth. Keep believing life is innately good, even when it doesn't feel that way. Hold on to the truth that no matter how unfair life has felt, you have the capacity within you to take what is still here and build something better than you would have

imagined. In doing all of this, the past becomes a valuable teacher rather than a burden, and you can view it as a stepping stone rather than something to trip over.

6. **Keep looking ahead.** Don't get stuck looking backward. You can look in only one direction at a time. Shift your attention to the present moment and its opportunities, look up to God, and look ahead in the direction you want to go. Ask Him to give you boldness to march into your new phase with hope, peace, and expectation in your heart. Engage in activities that bring you joy, and cultivate new interests. Follow that dream, and do what you know you can do. Be willing to take a chance on yourself and your God.

7. **Surround yourself with positive influences.** We all need support, especially when we trudge through difficult seasons. If you find it challenging to let go of the past on your own and you need help finding healing and peace, consider seeking support from a therapist, counselor, or support group. They can facilitate the healing process by providing guidance, tools, and a safe space to navigate your emotions. Spend time with people who believe in you and remind you that you're important and valued. People who support your biggest dreams and even your wildest visions for how you want your life to be. And don't spend time with those who don't do

that. Optimism is contagious, and so is pessimism. Choose your circle of friends and supporters wisely, and set boundaries where needed.

8. **Practice self-compassion.** Be kind to yourself throughout this process. You deserve it. Finding healing and wholeness, letting go of what once was, allowing yourself to be positive about the future when it's uncertain—that all takes time. Be patient and understanding with yourself. Give yourself the grace and love you would give a friend walking through a hard season.

9. **Stay focused on your goals.** Set your SMART goals; hold yourself accountable; celebrate your progress and your successes no matter how small. The dreams in your head, the vision of the life you want, an idea for a new adventure, the plan you have to start a new career, business, hobby—all are possible with SMART goals. Don't lose sight of your goals because life feels messy and not perfectly aligned. And remember, it's okay to have ups and downs along the way. To use a cliché you may have heard before, a setback is always a setup for a comeback in a divine way only God could orchestrate.

10. **Trust in your ability.** You've got this and God's got you. Saying goodbye to the past is a personal journey that will take time. Trust the process, have faith in your heavenly Father, and have confidence in your ability to create a brighter future.

It's time to get excited, my friend! It's time to stop dreaming about beginning again or doing that new thing or walking into the future with your head held high and start rolling up your sleeves and making it happen!

You may have heard this saying: "When one door closes, another door opens." But often we look so long and regretfully upon the closed door that we do not see the one that has opened for us. This is the space where dreams die. The space where God-opportunities are missed. The space where we overlook joys and new things because we're looking behind instead of ahead. The space where goals never get met because procrastination becomes a habit.

Never stop expecting and looking for the open doors. Don't just let life happen to you; make it happen for you. If you're not already leaning into your faith, start now.

Remember how Martin Luther King Jr. is reported to have said, "Take the first step in faith. You don't have to see the whole staircase, just take the first step."[1] That's exactly what we have to do when we embark on a new beginning. If we envision all the steps in front of us, we wonder if we can really make it to the top. The destination we desperately long to arrive at. But that's why goal setting is so important.

It gives us a strategy that paves the way, one step at a time. Your goals are the dream, and your steps are the subgoals that will get you there. In time, we will find ourselves looking at how far we've come rather than how far we still have to go.

You need to have faith in the process, but you also need to have faith in yourself. Faith that you can rise above what someone did to break your heart and shatter your dreams. Faith that you can make it through that situation that sent you to your knees—the medical diagnosis, the job loss, the financial setback, the loss of a loved one, the kids growing up, watching beloved parents age and decline, the rejection, the constant barrage of disappointments.

I promise: With faith in yourself and faith in your God, you've got this. You may not see it yet, and it may take a little longer to believe it (and maybe you need to read this book more than once for an extra dose of inspiration!), but you do have the strength within you through the power of Christ. Remember, "I can do everything through Christ, who gives me strength" (Phil. 4:13). This applies to you, not just everyone else.

Next, believe in your own resilience. Even if you feel weak and lost right now, you likely have more than you realize. God always gives us what we need, and you know what? He has already given you what you need to get through any lifequake.

Resilience is not only what you have inside you but also what you're willing to do to keep going. Given that you're here on earth, certainly you've been through some hard times. You've had your fair share of seasons when you felt lost and confused, faced with beginning again in some way—and maybe again and again. Yet you made it. Your internal fortitude got you through, and you still have the toughness to get through and rise above whatever you're facing right now. Pray for the conviction to get through it and the resilience to overcome it.

Amaze people with what you can do.

Amaze yourself.

Now It's Decision Time

Tony Robbins, a popular entrepreneur, number one *New York Times*–bestselling author, philanthropist, and life and business strategist, once said, "A real decision is measured by the fact that you've taken a new action. If there's no action, you haven't truly decided."[2] If you want a new beginning, decide right now to stop doing the same old things day after day, and start taking action to create your new path.

Have you decided to pull yourself up by your bootstraps and forge forth into your opportunities for beginning again? Are you ready to embark on that new path toward the future you want? If so, taking action is necessary for lighting that fire in your heart. Don't let that spark keep smoldering; give it the fuel of action.

Don't be opposed to small beginnings; they are moving you forward.

I know it's easier to set goals and dream about them than it is to take action. The thought of taking a deep plunge toward our goals can make us want to retreat. *What if I make a mistake? What if I fail?* All those what-ifs aren't our friends and will keep us stuck and uncomfortable, all the while longing for change but delaying getting started. Getting started can feel scary and paralyzing because you know if you start acting on your goals and ideas, then life will change.

But isn't that what you want? To walk out new beginnings and usher in the new with open arms, instead of just thinking about it or wishing for it? I know that's how it is for me, and I hope it is for you too. It's likely to feel overwhelming at first, but it can also be the most exciting and challenging time you've ever experienced. It might make you feel more alive than you've felt in a long time. And that's a good thing.

We are all capable of taking actions that will make us feel more vibrant, useful, and fulfilled. And you are no exception.

Say your goodbyes to what once was. Get the closure you need. Dust off your heart. Put a smile on your face. Set your goals and adjust them when needed. Celebrate every success that gets you a little closer to your dream. Keep your eyes on your vision. And don't be opposed to small beginnings; they are moving you forward.

Have faith in God. Have faith in yourself. Find your twenty seconds of insane courage and then some. Let your confidence grow. Be resilient. Make decisions. Start taking action and making this happen!

Then keep going.

Moving Forward

Think about It

What do you need to leave behind so you can open the door to your new beginning? Is it a place, a relationship, a job, a disappointment, a season, a pattern of thinking? Whatever it is, let it go. Say goodbye in whatever way makes it possible to close the door on the past, leave the hallway of the in-between, and trudge boldly through the open doors where exciting changes can begin taking shape. Give yourself closure and permission to begin moving forward.

Plan for It

Are you ready to do the work to make your dreams become reality? To see change start happening in yourself and in your life? I know you are! Think back to that declaration you made to yourself in chapter 9. Did you write it down?

As a refresher, making this declaration means you're not only resolving to try to meet your desires or thinking and dreaming about making something happen, and then if it does, it does, and if it doesn't, it doesn't. Instead, you're declaring to yourself once and for all that you will make things different going forward. You're proclaiming to yourself that you won't stop until you achieve your desires, and that is empowering. If you didn't write out your personal beginning-again declaration, then do that now!

Write out these great quotes about the value in planning, and keep them in places where you can routinely see them. Let them motivate you to keep planning for your future and making your dreams come true!

> An hour of planning can save you ten hours of doing. (Dale Carnegie Training, *Make Yourself Unforgettable*)

> A goal without a plan is just a wish. (Attributed to Antoine de Saint-Exupéry)

There are dreamers and there are planners; the planners make their dreams come true. (Attributed to Edwin Louis Cole)

The key is not to prioritize what's on your schedule, but to schedule your priorities. (Stephen R. Covey, *The 7 Habits of Highly Effective People*)

Plans are worthless, but planning is everything. (Dwight D. Eisenhower, November 14, 1957)

It takes as much time to wish as it does to plan. (Attributed to Eleanor Roosevelt)

If the plan doesn't work, change the plan, not the goal. (Anonymous)

Failing to plan is planning to fail. (Anonymous)

Act on It

Put into practice the ten tips from this chapter. Ponder each one, and pray for clarity on how to successfully navigate closure so you can begin welcoming new and positive changes into your life.

Let go of the past.
Embrace your emotions.
Give yourself closure.
Practice forgiveness.
View the past through a positive lens.
Leave the past in the past.
Surround yourself with positive influences.
Practice self-compassion.
Stay focused on your goals.
Trust in your ability.

Most importantly, start taking action today.
Your new beginning awaits!

Pray over It

Jesus, I'm excited at the thought of beginning again, and I want to start taking action and making changes in my life! I know that I can do this and that You've equipped me with dreams, hopes, and desires for my new beginning. I seek Your blessing on the plans and goals I will be pursuing and to be acutely aware of Your whispers and guidance along the way. Amen.

Write your own prayer to Jesus in this space.

Chapter 12

Time to Begin Again

Beginning again can mean different things to different people.

It's a personal journey, and there is no one-size-fits-all approach. As we pull into your destination station, where you get to hop off and run full force toward your new beginning, remember to trust yourself, be patient, and celebrate your progress along the way. But most of all, right now in this moment, accept the reality that it's time to begin again.

Although new beginnings can feel intimidating, we reap many benefits from accepting what is and embracing the adventure into the new.

First, our new beginnings provide opportunities for growth and development. Just like a little acorn that starts small and eventually grows into a mighty tree, our journeys may start small too. It may seem like we're not big enough or strong enough to make our dreams come true or overcome our difficult seasons. But every day, week, month, and year, like an oak tree that grows bigger and stronger despite the storms it endures, so will you.

Don't be opposed to small beginnings. Consider each act of faith and perseverance as proof you're growing, developing, and starting to blossom, even if you can't see it yet.

Second, consider the lessons you're learning along the way. Maybe this wasn't a journey you wanted to be on and you're struggling to move through this new phase of life. Or maybe you decided it was time to make a change and you're going for it with gusto. Either way, you'll learn valuable lessons through successes, setbacks, and failures. Each lesson shapes our character and prepares us for the blessings and the challenges that lie ahead.

Third, starting anew is the perfect time to focus on gratitude for what we have, for what God is doing in us, and for the progress we're making. It's a time we can cultivate a positive mindset and build confidence in God's faithfulness. By appreciating where we are right now, even if it's not where we want to be, we can find joy in the journey rather than focusing only on the destination.

Lastly, this is the perfect time to learn to fully rely on God. Beginning again reminds us of our dependence on Him. When we acknowledge our limitations, rely on Him, and continue to walk in faith toward our future, we open ourselves up to His guidance, strength, and provision.

Trusting God with your future requires recognizing that He is the ultimate source of your success. Never forget He can work wonders in any circumstance. Each time you see a huge tree looming overhead, pause. Take time to admire its strength, dignity, and beauty and consider how you are much like that beautiful, strong tree. Remember Psalm 40:2? It says, "He lifted me out of the pit of despair, out of the mud and the mire. He set my feet on solid ground and steadied me as I walked along." Stay on solid ground, and you'll continue to grow and bloom, season after season.

The Best Thing You Can Do for Yourself Is to Get Started

In the words of Joe Sabah, professional speaker, author, and publisher, "You don't have to be great to start, but you have to start to be great."[1]

No matter what we're facing or what lies behind us, we all must start somewhere.

We often want to skip from the start of a new beginning to the end, but remember that everyone started somewhere and that they got to where they are because they started. What we do in the beginning and middle of our journeys is what will determine where we arrive in the end.

With any goals or declarations we make, we must approach the starting line before the race can even begin. As you walk boldly into this exciting new chapter of life, here are a few reminders to help you get off on the right foot:

1. **Reflect on the past.** Take some time to remember the experiences and lessons you've gained from your previous endeavors and from life itself. Understand what worked well, what didn't, and what you want to change or improve on in the future. Rather than letting the past be something that holds you back, look at it as something to help propel you forward. Something that shaped you into who you are today. This self-reflection can provide valuable insights and guide your decision-making and your goal setting, as well as help you stay inspired to put in the effort to accomplish your dreams.

2. **Define your goals.** Determine what you want to achieve, as we talked about in chapter 9. Set clear SMART goals that align with your values and aspirations. Don't be afraid to dream big, but no matter what, dream. Whether your goals are related to your

personal life, your career, your relationships, your health, or any other category, having well-defined goals will help you stay focused and motivated.

3. **Create a plan.** Develop a detailed plan outlining the necessary steps to achieve your goals. Break down your objectives into smaller, actionable tasks, and set deadlines for each of them. This plan will serve as your road map and help you remain organized and accountable as you progress.

4. **Embrace change.** Beginning again requires accepting change and letting go of the past, but it also requires being open to new adventures and opportunities. It requires taking leaps of faith and trusting God with your future. Be willing to move outside your comfort zone, push your own boundaries, and explore different paths or approaches. Think outside the box, and embrace growth and adaptability, as they are essential for personal development.

5. **Dare to have those twenty seconds of insane courage.** Do something every day that fertilizes your confidence and helps it grow. Make a habit of being courageous even when something feels terrifying. Sometimes we simply must be braver than we want to be. Remember, your external bravery is what will catapult your internal confidence to a whole new level. Have courage. Build confidence.

6. **Take care of yourself.** You can't pour from an empty cup, so prioritizing self-care and well-being

throughout this process is crucial. Engage in activities that bring you joy, relaxation, and rejuvenation. Practice self-care techniques such as exercise, mindfulness, meditation, prayer, worship, hobbies, or any other strategies that prompt you to maintain a healthy balance physically, mentally, and emotionally. There is rarely anything stronger than a woman who has rebuilt herself and her life.

7. **Find your champions.** Don't hesitate to reach out to friends, family, or mentors who can provide guidance, encouragement, and support while you pursue your new beginnings. We all need people who believe in us. In addition to wise counsel and positive character influences, which are critical to have in your life, surrounding yourself with people who will be your champions no matter what and always support your endeavors in your journey of starting again is just as important. Don't let friends, family, or other well-meaning people talk you out of your dreams or goals. Even if they sound delusional to others, remember that it's your life and your vision, not anyone else's. Cheerleaders will always help you keep going! Find your team.

8. **Learn from setbacks.** Understand that setbacks and challenges are a natural part of any new beginning, but if we never risk failing, we'll never enjoy succeeding either. Instead of getting discouraged when mishaps or challenges roll in, ask God to help

you shift your perspective and view them as opportunities for growth and learning. Learn from your mistakes, adjust your approach if needed, and keep moving forward.

9. **Stay persistent and motivated.** Starting again can be a long and sometimes arduous process. Stay on course and committed to the declarations you made to yourself, even when faced with obstacles. Keep your motivation high by reminding yourself of the reasons you wanted to begin again in the first place. Give yourself permission to succeed and pursue your dreams. Own your value and own your purpose.

10. **Trust the process.** Because God is in it. And He's got you.

All these tips are so important, and getting started is key. But the day will come when you're tired and discouragement sets in. When you simply don't feel like trying anymore. Several years ago, when I found myself feeling exhausted with trying to rebuild my life, reinvent myself, and map out my path to new beginnings, I told God, "I can't do this anymore. I can't keep going. I give up. I'm tired of waiting to see how things will work out. I don't even know if all I'm doing is making a difference."

Maybe today you feel that way too. But upon uttering those words that day and admitting my weakness, I felt a nudge to my spirit, as if God tenderly placed His holy hand under my chin and tilted my head up. I lifted my eyes and immediately knew I needed to look up to God instead of around to my circumstances, my worries, and all the unknowns of the future.

I knew the vision and dreams He had given me for my future, and I needed to intentionally refocus on what He *had* done rather than what I felt He *had not* done yet. I needed to trust Him instead of doubting. I needed to stop thinking I had to fix everything on my own and trust the only One who actually could.

During the remainder of that day, as I tried to adjust my focus, hope and peace slowly began to return. Thankfully, I didn't throw in the towel, and I'm so glad God continued to fuel me with what I needed every day to keep gaining ground.

Through faith alone, I had chosen to God-up rather than give up. Not because I had the strength to do so, but because I had God's strength within me to keep pushing forward in faith, much like Paul did in biblical times.

There is rarely anything stronger than a woman who has rebuilt herself and her life.

In 2 Corinthians 4, Paul encouraged the church of Corinth to press on. He reminded the people they all held a treasure in their hearts—the Spirit of God—which was the sole reason they could stay steadfast when they felt like quitting in the face of adversities, especially when it came to defending the gospel.

In verse 1—"Since God in his mercy has given us this new way, we never give up"—we see proof of the fact that although he stumbled in his faith at times, Paul consistently kept his eyes focused on God. The "new way" he was referring to is that we can all freely enjoy the gift of grace, mercy, hope, and strength because of God's Spirit within us, rather than having to follow rules and regulations to try to earn His favor (the Old Testament way). Every time Paul wanted to give up, he essentially chose to God-up instead. He routinely chose to depend on God's power instead of his own.

Knowing Jesus was his Savior always equipped and inspired Paul to keep from quitting even when he had every earthly, common-sense reason to do so. The truth is, he suffered more than any one person should have to suffer and likely more than we ever will. Over his lifetime, he was imprisoned, beaten, stoned, shipwrecked, and chased mercilessly by enemies. He suffered mental and spiritual exhaustion in addition to physical pain, hunger, thirst, difficult living conditions, and even a lack of clothing at times. If you ask me, that's enough to make anyone want to give up! Yet despite his weakest moments, he never did.

The choice Paul made day after day to God-up instead of giving up filled him with strength and perseverance he never could have found on his own. I can only assume that as you travel this new path, there will be times when your faith is weak. When you think you can't go on. When you don't feel courageous at all, much less confident. When thinking about all it will take to reinvent yourself and your life seems overwhelming. When you want to give up too. But please don't.

Everyone struggles with those thoughts and feelings from time to time. But, like Paul, the moment we catch ourselves feeling that way is the very moment we're faced with the choice to God-up or give up. And the only ones who succeed at reaching their goals are the ones who choose to keep going.

Live with No Regrets

When we God-up instead of giving up, God will always show up. And He will show up for you!

Beginning again isn't always easy. Yet to put things in perspective, the opposite of beginning again is staying stuck in a situation or season, never embracing change, missing out on the opportunities and blessings God has in store for us when we trust Him, and then most likely regretting it.

I shared about Bronnie Ware in my book *Love Life Again: Finding Joy When Life Is Hard*, but I think her findings are so relevant, I wanted to share them again here.

Bronnie, an Australian nurse, spent several years caring for patients with terminal illnesses in the last weeks of their lives, sort of like a hospice nurse. She kept a diary of all the regrets people said they had when they were nearing the end of their lives and eventually turned it into an article and then a book called *The Top Five Regrets of the Dying*. More than three million people around the globe read the article in the year after it was released.[2]

Bronnie came face to face with the reality that we can all enjoy life if we make enjoying it a priority. In her book, she wrote that among all the regrets people shared with her at the end of their lives, some things were mentioned again and again. The first was that people wished they had lived a life truer to themselves rather than always trying to meet the expectations of others or worrying about what other people thought. Second, they wished they hadn't worked so hard, and this was especially common for men. Third, people wished they had been more open about their feelings, followed by the fourth regret of wishing they had stayed more in touch with friends and made time for the important people in their lives.[3]

The last most commonly stated regret was that people wished they had allowed themselves to be happier.

Bronnie wrote, "Many did not realise until the end that happiness is a choice. They had stayed stuck in old patterns and habits. The so-called 'comfort' of familiarity overflowed into their emotions, as well as their physical lives. Fear of change had them pretending to others, and to [themselves], that they were content. When deep within, they longed to laugh properly and have silliness in their life again."[4]

If life has been hard for you and you feel like you're drowning in this transitional period, I bet your heart is longing to laugh and be silly again. Do you look forward to feeling lighthearted and less burdened again? Are you hungering for peace? Can you feel that twinge of anticipation in your spirit, knowing you're on the brink of something awesome? It can happen! It's my prayer that this book has given you hope that you can feel that way very, very soon if you God-up, make personal declarations, make decisions and plans, and then take action to start turning your visions of a better future into reality.

Another truth I shared in my book *Love Life Again* is that if there is one thing for certain, it's that our days are numbered, no matter how old we are or what season of life we are in. We can't change the past or get back all those days we wasted feeling unhappy and discontent with the lives God has given us.[5] We don't get a do-over for all the time we wasted being afraid to embrace a new beginning or even give God a chance to show us what He can do.

Yet we can choose to start living differently today and put into practice the ten tips from this chapter and all the other tips, tools, and strategies outlined in this book. We also need to make a commitment to keep going because it's all too easy to procrastinate while time quickly slips away.

Another powerful observation comes from Swiss American psychiatrist and pioneer of studies on dying people, Elisabeth Kübler-Ross, who wrote a book titled *Death: The Final Stage of Growth*. In this book published in 1975, she said, "It is the denial of death that is partially responsible for people living empty, purposeless lives; for when you live as if you'll live forever, it becomes too easy to postpone the things you know that you must do."[6]

Harvard psychology professor Daniel Gilbert wrote a popular book titled *Stumbling on Happiness*, where he referenced studies about taking action in our lives. He said, "In the long run, people of every age and in every walk of life seem to regret *not* having done things much more than they regret things they *did*."[7] It's easier on our hearts and minds to tap into our courage rather than our cowardice, so why not take a chance on ourselves today and pursue our wildest dreams?

We also can embrace a new attitude and outlook, which will help shape our future. It's been said, "In the end, it's not the years in your life that count. It's the life in your years." You have life right now. This is your one life to live. You don't have to live one more day or one more minute feeling stuck in this transition period, afraid of striving for where you want to be. You can begin your new beginning today.

As proven by Bronnie Ware's work and maybe by people you've known, there's something even scarier than embracing new beginnings, living with unshakable optimism about what the future holds, and making your joy a priority, and that is getting to the end of your life with regrets. When our lives are defined by other people, lies from the Enemy, limiting beliefs, doubts, fears, a lack of self-worth, a lack of confidence and bravery, and an unwillingness to trust God in the face of new beginnings and hard circumstances, we're robbed of possibilities we could have embraced, experiences we could have enjoyed, and successes and joy we could have achieved.

We Can't Change the Past, but We Can Change the Future

Isaiah 65:17 prompts us to let go of the past and embrace new seasons, just like God does: "See, I will create new heavens and a new earth. The former things will not be remembered, nor will they come to mind" (NIV). Anything we can't change or control is something we need to let go.

God doesn't remember our mistakes and failures, and letting go of our grip on the past frees us up to reach for the future. Isaiah 43:18–19 reminds us, "Forget all that—it is nothing compared to what I am going to do. For I am about to do something new. See, I have already begun! Do you not see it? I will make a pathway through the wilderness. I will create rivers in the dry wasteland."

Ecclesiastes 3:1–8 says,

> For everything there is a season,
>   a time for every activity under heaven.
> A time to be born and a time to die.
>   A time to plant and a time to harvest.
> A time to kill and a time to heal.
>   A time to tear down and a time to build up.

A time to cry and a time to laugh.

A time to grieve and a time to dance.

A time to scatter stones and a time to gather stones.

A time to embrace and a time to turn away.

A time to search and a time to quit searching.

A time to keep and a time to throw away.

A time to tear and a time to mend.

A time to be quiet and a time to speak.

A time to love and a time to hate.

A time for war and a time for peace.

This passage reminds us that life is wonderfully measured in seasons, which we will all experience, and that God is in every season and always in the details.

Psalm 40:3 also should inspire us about our new beginnings: "He put a new song in my mouth, a hymn of praise to our God. Many will see and fear the LORD and put their trust in him" (NIV). The Psalms are full of praise and singing new songs to the Lord. Whenever we find ourselves in a scary place, facing unknowns, we can sing a new song of praise to our heavenly Father. Praise is an amazing weapon against the Enemy, who wants to keep us down, and fear, which prevents us from pressing forward.

The Bible consistently stresses the value of patience, which is a significant virtue to have when starting anything new and waiting for good changes to happen. Lamentations 3:22–24 is one such passage: "Because of the LORD's great love we are not consumed, for his compassions never fail. They are new every morning; great is your faithfulness. I say to myself, 'The LORD is my portion; therefore I will wait for him'" (NIV).

In this passage, we see the hope of a new morning. New mercies. Fresh beginnings. God's compassions are new every day; therefore each day of our journey can start out with fresh hope, no matter what the day before held. God is always at work, and patience prepares us to one day see evidence of His work with our own eyes.

Proverbs 3:5–6 says, "Trust in the LORD with all your heart; do not depend on your own understanding. Seek his will in all you do, and he will show you which path to take." Trusting in God is the foundation that allows us to begin building our new life.

Our new beginnings can start right where we are. God has already given us everything we need to start anew: experience, wisdom, lessons learned, faith, blessings, talents, skills, and so much more. A new beginning lies ahead for anyone who is willing and desiring to make Jesus the Lord of their life. Second Corinthians 5:17 says, "Anyone who belongs to Christ has become a new person. The old life is gone; a new life has begun!" If we place our hope in the fact that we have a new beginning in Christ, we should certainly feel equipped to embrace any other new beginning.

Perseverance is the pathway to new beginnings because progress, change, and success take time and require patience. The translation of James 5:10–11 in *The Message* provides great motivation for persevering: "Take the old prophets as your mentors. They put up with anything, went through everything, and never once quit, all the time honoring God. What a gift life is to those who stay the course! You've heard, of course, of Job's staying power, and you know how God brought it all together for him at the end. That's because God cares, cares right down to the last detail."

Job went through long seasons of pain and hardship, yet he trusted God, and God paved the way for an entirely new beginning and restored everything he had lost. Although different from Job's suffering, our seasons of hardship and waiting can feel like forever. We may want to give up and assume nothing will ever change and good can never come. But staying the course is what will help us have a new beginning and, in time, change the trajectory of our lives.

Last but certainly not least, remember that the end of a thing is often more valuable than the beginning of it. Ecclesiastes 7:8 says, "Finishing is better than starting. Patience is better than pride." *The Message* paraphrases that verse this way: "Endings are better than beginnings. Sticking to it is better than standing out." The King James Version reads, "Better is the end of a thing than the beginning thereof: and the patient in spirit is better than the proud in spirit," and the New Century Version says, "It is better to finish something than to start it. It is better to be patient than to be proud."

All these verses can be our daily inspiration not only to get started with our new beginnings but also to let go of the past, have patience, trust God, and maintain hope and optimism. And just as importantly, to always keep running and finish the race well!

Starting something new and seeing our visions and dreams begin to take shape is one of the best feelings in the world. Seeing success, or simply seeing progress, boosts our self-esteem, increases our confidence and courage, gives us space in our heads to think clearly about what we need to do next, and therefore helps open the door to more possibilities.

Seeing progress also gives us momentum to keep going! You take step after step, and before you know it, you're somewhere you never thought you'd be! But finishing is even better.

What is your vision for your new life? Write it down. Create a vision board. Set your goals. Prepare your heart. Get excited. Forge ahead with a vow to never give up. And trust wholeheartedly that God has a great plan for you, like Jeremiah 29:11 says. Whatever your age, situation, or season of life, regardless of what failures or setbacks you've experienced, decide right this very moment that you will take action to create the life and future you want and never settle for anything less.

One of my favorite movies from years gone by was *Facing the Giants*, a 2006 Sherwood Pictures production centered on overcoming fear with faith. It was directed by Alex Kendrick and was quite a hit at the box office for a low-budget film. My children and I watched it over and over. Not only because I'm an avid football fan, but also because of the enormous faith lessons tucked into practically every scene.

There are countless powerful quotes from the movie, but one of my very favorites was when Grant Taylor, the main character and coach of a football team that had given up hope of ever being champions, said, "Whether you make this field goal or not, we're gonna praise Him. But don't you walk off this field having done any less than your best."[8]

If you're going to do this thing—this act of beginning again—never give it anything less than your best.

Whatever you have your sights on, never cease to give it your all. Don't give up. Make a commitment that no matter what happens, you will always give yourself and your God your very best. Give your new beginnings the best of who you are, and above all else, always praise Him.

Let the future pique your curiosity. Tap into that courage you've been building up. Let your confidence grow. Seek out your biggest cheerleaders to keep you going. And remember that, even in the face of uncertainties, everything is possible with Jesus Christ.

Finally, don't be afraid to begin again. You never know—you may like your new story even better. And a year from now, you're going to be so glad you didn't give up! You have no idea how amazing life is about to get if you stay focused and trust the process. You just might be walking into the chapter of life you've been waiting for.

You've got this because God's got you.

It's time to begin again, my friend. So begin.

Moving Forward

Think about It

What is your definition of beginning again? Write it out on a piece of paper. This is for your eyes only. Allow yourself to think through and write down your feelings, your fears, your desires, your reasons for hesitation, what you need to let go and what you need to embrace, if you need to work on shifting your perspective and thinking patterns, and so on. Let this serve as your motivation to push past all your obstacles and truly embrace your season of beginning again.

Also, think about what you might regret if you don't begin again. If nothing else, let that be the fuel you need to set a fire in your heart to give your new beginning a fighting chance. Invite happiness and joy into your life, and expect it to happen.

Plan for It

Think of yourself as that little acorn that is just beginning to sprout into an oak tree. How do you want to see yourself grow? What would make you happiest if it came to fruition? How quickly do you want to see growth and changes beginning to happen, and what do you need to do right now to start watering those dreams?

What are the lessons you've learned throughout your lifetime that have equipped and prepared you for such a time as this? How can you plan to apply those lessons to your goals?

Make a list of the blessings you can be grateful for—all the things God has done in your life. Use this as a daily reminder that He has been at work your entire life and will continue to work on answering your deepest prayers in the invisible realms. And each time He does, add it to your list, and keep a running tally of your reasons to be grateful! A grateful heart is always a happy heart.

Stay in God's Word, and spend time in prayer, especially on days when you feel like giving up. He is there for us to lean on, so lean on Him.

Act on It

Look back at your notes and journaling as you worked through this book, revisit your dreams and visions for your future, review your goals, make sure you have all your action steps in place, and make a move! Refuse to allow yourself to procrastinate. Let today be the first day of your new beginning. This is your time. Go for it because you've got this! Just. Get. Started. And never ever give up!

Pray over It

Jesus, Lord, I'm ready to embark on my new beginning! Infuse me with strength, courage, confidence, creativity, curiosity, and insight into the specific steps I need to take to make my dreams come true. I trust that You will be leading me throughout this new journey, and I commit to trust You no matter what! Help me push past setbacks and disappointments and never give up but instead look up to You for everything I need. Thank You for loving me and for hearing my prayers. I love You, Lord, and each time I'm in the position of beginning again, I will remember that You love me and You are with me. I believe You've got me and my life in Your hands, so thanks to You, I've got this. Amen.

Write your own prayer to Jesus in this space.

Notes

Chapter 3: Keep Your Eyes on the Horizon

1. Adi Jaffe, "Podcast 125: Overcoming Addiction with Dr. Adi Jaffe," interview by Caroline Leaf, *Cleaning Up the Mental Mess*, January 29, 2020, www.youtube.com /watch?v=mWWWbkdC0GU.

Chapter 4: The Power of a Thought

1. Karen Kaiser Clark, *Life Is Change—Growth Is Optional* (Saint Paul, MN: Center for Executive Planning, 1998).

2. Joyce Meyer, *Approval Addiction: Overcoming Your Need to Please Everyone* (New York: Warner Faith, 2005), 114.

Chapter 5: Understanding Transitions and Mistakes to Avoid

1. Dictionary.com, s.v. "transition," accessed November 5, 2023, www.dictionary .com/browse/transition.

2. Gemma Brown, "Understanding the Four Types of Life Transition," Gemma Brown Coaching, last modified July 25, 2023, www.gemmabrowncoaching.co.uk /post/understanding-life-transitions.

3. *Merriam-Webster*, s.v. "surrender," accessed December 20, 2023, www.merriam-webster.com/dictionary/surrender.

Chapter 6: The Key to Transitioning Well

1. BetterHelp Editorial Team, "Transform Your Life: Understanding the Signs of Low Self-Esteem," BetterHelp, last modified January 22, 2024, www.betterhelp .com/advice/self-esteem/signs-of-low-self-esteem-and-what-to-do-about-it.

2. "Self-Esteem," Counseling and Mental Health Center, University of Texas at Austin, accessed November 6, 2023, https://cmhc.utexas.edu/selfesteem.html.

3. Lysa TerKeurst, "The Breath of Fresh Air Your Heart Has Been Asking For," Lysa TerKeurst, September 13, 2023, https://lysaterkeurst.com/2023/09/13 /the-breath-of-fresh-air-your-heart-has-been-asking-for (emphasis added).

4. "The Connection between Helping Others and Your Health," Behavioral Health Systems, August 1, 2019, https://behavioralhealthsystems.com/connection-helping -others-health.

Chapter 7: With Courage Comes Confidence

1. *We Bought a Zoo*, directed by Cameron Crowe (Los Angeles, CA: Twentieth Century Fox, 2011).

2. Diana Ross, quoted in "Words of the Week," *Jet*, February 4, 1985, 40.

Chapter 8: Time to Adopt a New Perspective

1. "About Marie Kondo," KonMari, accessed November 8, 2023, https://konmari .com/about-marie-kondo.

2. Marie Kondo, quoted in Jura Koncius, "Marie Kondo's Life Is Messier Now—and She's Fine with It," *Washington Post*, January 26, 2023, www.washingtonpost.com /home/2023/01/26/marie-kondo-kurashi-inner-calm.

Chapter 9: Time to Start Planning

1. "What Makes a Goal 'S.M.A.R.T'?," Wisconsin Department of Public Instruction, accessed February 28, 2024, https://dpi.wi.gov/sites/default/files/imce/acp/SMART %20goals.pdf.

2. Gail Matthews, quoted in Sarah Gardner and Dave Albee, "Study Focuses on Strategies for Achieving Goals, Resolutions," Dominican University of California, February 1, 2015, https://scholar.dominican.edu/news-releases/266.

3. "Fun Facts about New Year's Resolutions," LifeProtect 24/7, accessed January 31, 2024, https://lifeprotect247.com/blog/fun-facts-new-years-resolutions.

4. Dictionary.com, s.v. "resolution," accessed November 9, 2023, www.dictionary .com/browse/resolution.

5. Dictionary.com, s.v. "declaration," accessed November 9, 2023, www.dictionary .com/browse/declaration.

6. George T. Doran, "There's a S.M.A.R.T. Way to Write Management's Goals and Objectives," *Management Review* (November 1981): 35–36.

7. Margie Warrell, *You've Got This! The Life-Changing Power of Trusting Yourself* (Brisbane, Australia: John Wiley & Sons, 2020), 148.

8. Joel Arthur Barker, quoted in *Oxford Essential Quotations*, ed. Susan Ratcliffe, 4th ed. (Oxford: Oxford University Press, 2016), www.oxfordreference.com /display/10.1093/acref/9780191826719.001.0001/q-oro-ed4-00011987.

Chapter 10: Time to Start Trusting

1. *365 Days of Hope & Encouragement: An Inspirational DaySpring DayBrightener—Perpetual Calendar* (Siloam Springs, AR: DaySpring), June 7, 2022.

2. Margie Warrell, *You've Got This! The Life-Changing Power of Trusting Yourself* (Brisbane, Australia: John Wiley & Sons, 2020), 50.

Chapter 11: Time to Say Goodbye to What Was

1. Martin Luther King Jr., quoted by Marian Wright Edelman in *Mother Jones Magazine*, May–June 1991, Foundation for National Progress, 77.

2. Tony Robbins, Facebook, May 19, 2021, www.facebook.com/TonyRobbins/photos/a.444057769059/10159624443854060.

Chapter 12: Time to Begin Again

1. Joe Sabah, quoted in Zig Ziglar, *Over the Top: Moving from Survival to Stability, from Stability to Success, from Success to Significance*, rev. ed. (Nashville, TN: Thomas Nelson, 1997), 8.

2. "Top Five Regrets of the Dying: A Life Transformed by the Dearly Departing," Barnes and Noble, accessed November 15, 2023, www.barnesandnoble.com/w/the-top-five-regrets-of-the-dying-bronnie-ware/1105496434.

3. Bronnie Ware, *The Top Five Regrets of the Dying: A Life Transformed by the Dearly Departing* (London: Hay House, 2012).

4. Bronnie Ware, "Top 5 Regrets of the Dying," *HuffPost*, January 21, 2012, www.huffpost.com/entry/top-5-regrets-of-the-dyin_b_1220965.

5. Tracie Miles, *Love Life Again: Finding Joy When Life Is Hard* (Colorado Springs, CO: David C Cook, 2018), 215.

6. Elisabeth Kübler-Ross, *Death: The Final Stage of Growth* (New York: Touchstone, 1986), 164.

7. Daniel Gilbert, *Stumbling on Happiness* (New York: Alfred A. Knopf, 2006), 179.

8. *Facing the Giants*, directed by Alex Kendrick (Albany, GA: Sherwood Pictures, 2006).

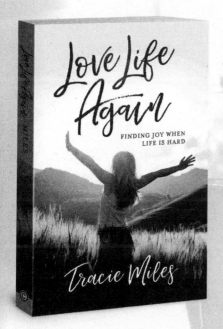

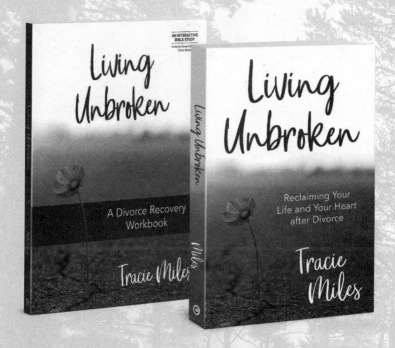

Your Marriage May Be Broken But You Don't Have to Be

In the *Living Unbroken* series, drawing from her own experience with divorce, Tracie Miles addresses the heartbreak of loss that comes from the breakup of a marriage while providing practical tips and guidance to women for overcoming the belief they will never be happy again, dispelling the myth that divorce can't be Christian, and teaching scriptural truths to help women embrace renewed purpose and joy.

Available in print and digital
wherever books are sold

estherpress